Kansas Bucket List Adventure Guide

Explore 100 Offbeat Destinations You Must Visit!

Douglas Huber

Canyon Press
canyon@purplelink.org

Please consider writing a review!
Just visit: purplelink.org/review

ISBN: 978-1-957590-07-3

FREE BONUS

Discover 31 Incredible Places You Can
Visit Next! Just Go To:

purplelink.org/travel

Table of Contents

How to Use This Book

Welcome to your very own adventure guide to exploring the many wonders of the state of Kansas. Not only does this book offer the most wonderful places to visit and sights to see in the vast state, but it provides GPS coordinates for Google Maps to make exploring that much easier.

Adventure Guide
Sorted by region, this guide offers over 100 amazing wonders found in Kansas for you to see and explore. They can be visited in any order, and this book will help you keep track of where you've been and where to look forward to going next. Each section describes the area or place, what to look for, how to get there, and what you may need to bring along.

GPS Coordinates
As you can imagine, not all of the locations in this book have a physical address. Fortunately, some of our listed wonders are either located within a National Park or Reserve or near a city, town, or place of business. For those that are not associated with a specific location, it is easiest to map it using GPS coordinates.

Luckily, Google has a system of codes that converts the coordinates into pin-drop locations that Google Maps can interpret and navigate.

Each adventure in this guide includes GPS coordinates along with a physical address whenever it is available.

It is important that you are prepared for poor cell signals. It is recommended that you route your location and ensure that the directions are accessible offline. Depending on your device and the distance of some locations, you may need to travel with a backup battery source.

About Kansas

Kansas, also known as the Sunflower State, joined the Union in 1861 as the 24th state. However, people have lived in the area for at least 12,200 years. Native American tribes such as the Kansa, Pawnee, Comanche, Osage, and Kiowa settled in Kansas well before the first European explorer, Francisco Vasquez, came in 1541 in search of a city made of gold. He didn't find what he was looking for, but other Europeans followed his path, including French explorers and fur-traders in the 1700s.

The U.S. eventually acquired the Kansas territory from France in 1803 as part of the Louisiana Purchase. In 1854, Kansas residents were allowed to vote on whether or not to become a slave state as part of the Kansas–Nebraska Act. Kansas eventually entered the U.S. as a free state, but in the same year it was admitted, the Civil War began, causing a major rift between slave and free states.

Kansas is named for the Kansa Native American tribe, and the word *Kansa* means "People of the South Wind." However, some Kansas residents call themselves Jayhawks, after bands of robbers who roamed the fields before the Civil War. However, after the war began, many Jayhawks enlisted in the military and fought for the Union and abolition. The University of Kansas, located in Lawrence, continues this tradition with their mascot, the Jayhawks.

The nickname for Kansas, the Sunflower State, is derived from the fields of sunflowers that grow along the plains. The farmland upon which sunflowers and other crops are planted provides the state with its top natural resource. Despite the number of sunflower fields, the state's largest crop is wheat, which has given rise to Kansas's title as the Wheat Capital of the World.

The capital of Kansas is Topeka, but its most populated city is Wichita. Topeka is located near the Kansas River, which gave it a strategic position during the Civil War. That's one of the main reasons why it was chosen to be the capital city of this state. Another reason, of course, is that the river provided the potential for significant economic growth.

Landscape and Climate

Kansas is one of the flattest states in the country, but there are some gentle hills in the Dissected Till Plains, which are located in the northeastern part of the state. This land was dissected into hills more than 400,000 years ago when moving glaciers and wind-carved the valleys and prominences you see today. Traveling south, you'll find the Southeastern Plains, including the Osage Plains, which are comprised of shale and limestone. The Flint Hills are also there, which are named for the erosion-resistant flint ridges.

The Great Plains are to the west. The area rises steadily in elevation as you work your way toward the Rocky Mountains in Colorado. As you approach the border between Kansas and Colorado, you'll see Mount Sunflower, which, at 4,039 feet tall, is the highest point in Kansas. Along with Colorado to the west, Kansas is bordered by Nebraska in the north, Oklahoma in the south, and Missouri in the east. It shares a major city, Kansas City, with Missouri.

Among the wildlife you'll see in Kansas are shrews, black-tailed jackrabbits, nine-banded armadillos, Great Plains skinks, prairie lizards, western meadowlarks, prairie chickens, golden eagles, western worm snakes, prairie king snakes, black vultures, and yellow-billed cuckoos. While the northeastern portion of Kansas boasts crops of cottonwood, cedar, maple, oak, and walnut trees, the main vegetation in the state is grass. Buffalo, bluestem, switch, Indian, and bluegrass are the most prominent grasses in the area.

The climate in Kansas is temperate, but there are extreme temperatures between summer and winter. July is the hottest month, coming in with average high temperatures of 81°F, and January is the coldest, with average temperatures hovering around 31°F. While the eastern part of the state can see upwards of 40 inches of precipitation, the west is distinctly drier. Snow and ice are common in the winter, and there's rain in the spring. Droughts can be a concern in the summer. Humidity can also make an appearance the further east you go, but it's not as noticeable as it is in eastern and southern states.

Dwight D. Eisenhower Library, Museum & Boyhood Home

Every U.S. president has the opportunity to establish a library and museum that tells the story of their life and time in the White House. Dwight D. Eisenhower, the 34th president of the United States, elected to have his built in his boyhood hometown of Abilene. The goal of this museum is to promote the public understanding of the highest office in the land and the American experience. In this library and museum, you'll discover approximately 26 million pages of historical documents, 768,000 feet of film, 335,000 photographs, and 70,000 artifacts. You can also tour the 19th-century home in which the Eisenhower family lived between 1898 and 1946. Dwight D. Eisenhower was one of a family of eight (and, later, a grandfather) who lived in this six-room house. The home was opened for tours in 1947.

Best Time to Visit: The museum is typically open Wednesday through Saturday from 10:00 a.m. to 2:00 p.m.

Pass/Permit/Fees: Adult admission is $15 per person. Senior admission for visitors ages 62 and older is $12, and student admission is $10 per person.

Closest City or Town: Abilene

Address: 200 SE 4th St., Abilene, KS 67410

GPS Coordinates: 38.91193° N, 97.21085° W

Did You Know? Dwight D. Eisenhower is the only 5-star general to become a U.S. president.

Amelia Earhart Birthplace Museum

The house that would become Amelia Earhart's birthplace was constructed in 1861, but the future aviator wasn't born there until 1897. Even though Earhart and her family lived in several cities as she grew up, she always considered Atchison her hometown. After all, she spent more time in the wood-frame Gothic Revival structure during her childhood than anywhere else.

This museum is one of the few remaining links to Earhart. While the world knows Earhart as a famous female pilot, one who disappeared in mysterious fashion during a flight, she was also a wife, stepmom, daughter, sister, friend, airline owner, clothes designer, author, photographer, college advisor, and much more.

Best Time to Visit: The museum is open Tuesday through Thursday from 10:00 a.m. to 2:00 p.m. and Friday and Saturday from 10:00 a.m. to 4:00 p.m. The last tour begins 45 minutes before closing.

Pass/Permit/Fees: Adult admission is $8. Military members and children between the ages of 5 and 12 are $4. Seniors are $6, and children under age 4 are free.

Closest City or Town: Atchison

Address: 223 N. Terrace St., Atchison, KS 6002

GPS Coordinates: 36.56454° N, 95.11431° W

Did You Know? Amelia Earhart's depiction in a Lucky Strike cigarettes advertisement, which is on display at the museum, lost her several endorsements.

Baker Wetlands

This 927-acre area of wetlands on the campus of Baker University is home to 278 bird species, ninety-eight other vertebrate species, and 487 plant species. With each exploration, these numbers grow as new species are identified. The wetlands represent one of the most diverse habitats in the state and provide Baker University students with biological and ecological educational opportunities that aren't available anywhere else. While the wetlands provide a superior learning experience for students, they aren't the only ones who use the area. Birdwatchers, hikers, stargazers, and nature lovers frequent the wetlands to enjoy the diverse fauna and peaceful environment. There are more than 11 miles of hiking trails throughout the wetlands that are open daily from dawn to dusk.

Best Time to Visit: The best time to visit is during the spring or fall when the weather is cooler.

Pass/Permit/Fees: There is no fee to visit this area.

Closest City or Town: Baldwin City

Address: 1365 N 1250 Rd, Lawrence, KS 66046

GPS Coordinates: 38.92258° N, 95.23555° W

Did You Know? Originally, the Baker Wetlands were used to teach farming to Haskell Institute students, but the land was given to Baker University by the Department of Health, Education, and Welfare in 1968 as a conservation project.

Prairie Lavender Farm

While there are numerous lavender fields in eastern Kansas, Prairie Lavender Farm is one that not only appreciates visitors but welcomes them as well.

The farm is dedicated to producing small batches of handmade lavender products to ensure the highest quality possible and provide these items at a reasonable price to customers. It opened in 2002 and is situated between the tallgrass and shortgrass prairies in Kansas.

Prairie Lavender Farm's exceptional location on the south side of a sandstone shelf above the Dakota Aquifer provides superior drainage for its lavender plants. More than 4,600 plants are grown on the farm, including a dozen lavender varieties.

Best Time to Visit: The best time to visit Prairie Lavender Farm is in late spring and early summer when the lavender is in bloom. The farm is open Wednesday through Saturday in June and July from 9:00 a.m. to 12:00 p.m.

Pass/Permit/Fees: There is no fee to visit Prairie Lavender Farm, but be sure to bring money for purchases.

Closest City or Town: Bennington

Address: 69 Alpine Ridge Ln., Bennington, KS 67422

GPS Coordinates: 38.96830° N, 97.62819

Did You Know? If you're unable to make it to the farm, look for Prairie Lavender Farm products at many local stores throughout Kansas.

Mushroom Rock State Park

As a stop on the Prairie Trail Scenic Byway, Mushroom Rock State Park provides visitors the opportunity to view one of the Eight Wonders of Kansas Geography during their bucolic drive. Mushroom Rock State Park may be the smallest state park in Kansas, but its unusual rock formations make it one of the most interesting.

Although just 5 acres in size, you'll experience the unique rocks that served as a meeting place and landmark for both early pioneers and Native Americans. Explorers John C. Fremont and Kit Carson both referenced Mushroom Rock during their travels.

The rock formations, which resemble giant mushrooms rising above the plains, consist of sandstone, sedimentary rock, and calcium carbonate. They were formed between 66 and 144 million years ago during the Cretaceous Period.

Best Time to Visit: The best time to visit is during the spring or fall when the weather is cooler.

Pass/Permit/Fees: There is no fee to visit this area.

Closest City or Town: Brookville

Address: Avenue K, Brookville, KS 67425

GPS Coordinates: 38.72742° N, 98.03064° W

Did You Know? The largest mushroom rock in the park is 27 feet in diameter. There are many more rock formations in the area, but they are buried under the surrounding soil.

Safari Zoological Park

Most zoos do not allow you to touch the animals that live in their habitats, but that's not how Safari Zoological Park operates. You can get up close and personal with a variety of animals here, including primates, kangaroo joeys, baby alligators, snakes, lemurs, and hedgehogs. Other animals may also be available depending on which animals have been born recently when you visit. Of course, you won't be able to interact with the adult animals, but the baby versions are sweet and playful. The owners, Tom and Allie Harvey, put the welfare of the animals in their park at the forefront of their operations to ensure they are safe and content. While you can tour the facility without interacting with the animals, the VIP package allows you to engage with numerous species that you normally wouldn't see in your everyday environment.

Best Time to Visit: The park is open Monday through Saturday from 10:00 a.m. to 2:00 p.m., and the last tour starts at 1:30 p.m. If the weather is bad or extremely hot, the park will not open, so always call first.

Pass/Permit/Fees: Adult admission is $14.95. Children ages 2-12 and seniors over 60 cost $12.95. Children under the age of 2 are free.

Closest City or Town: Caney

Address: 1751 County Rd. 1425, Caney, KS 67333

GPS Coordinates: 37.01385° N, 95.90089° W

Did You Know? Admission includes one hour at the Tree House and swimming pool.

Maxwell Wildlife Refuge

Visitors to Maxwell Wildlife Refuge can catch a glimpse of about fifty elk and 200 bison, helping them imagine what the plains were like 200 years ago. A road is available to take visitors through the refuge, where they may even get an up-close experience with one of these incredible animals. However, you should always remain safely inside your vehicle if you're in the open-range section of the park. To scan the hills for wildlife, climb the observation tower, which overlooks the refuge. Nearby McPherson State Fishing Lake is an excellent place to view stunning displays of wildflowers, including purple prairie clover, coneflowers, yucca, yellow star grass, spiderwort, catclaw sensitive brier, and even the rare goat's rue.

Best Time to Visit: Between mid-September and mid-October, the elk in the refuge will be breeding, and you'll be able to hear their majestic bugling in the mornings and evenings.

Pass/Permit/Fees: There is no fee to visit the Maxwell Wildlife Refuge unless you want a private tour on Saturdays.

Closest City or Town: Canton

Address: 2565 Pueblo Rd., Canton, KS 67428

GPS Coordinates: 38.47148° N, 97.45282° W

Did You Know? Due to the abundant butterfly milkwood in the refuge, you're likely to see numerous butterflies during your visit, including the rare regal fritillary.

The World's Largest Ball of Twine

In 1953, farmer Frank Stoeber began rolling twine from his hay bales into a ball rather than sweeping it up and burning it. After three years of doing this, the ball weighed 2 tons and was 7 feet high. Neighbors began bringing their twine to Frank to add to his ball, and Frank kept meticulous records about the ball's growth and weight. He also kept a notebook that contained the names of everyone who had given him twine.

In 1961, Frank was running out of room to keep the twine ball in his barn, so he removed it and put it in the Cawker City Centennial Parade. It was so popular that it was then moved to a concrete slab near the highway, where it remains today.

Best Time to Visit: The best time to visit the World's Largest Ball of Twine is during daylight hours.

Pass/Permit/Fees: There is no fee to visit this attraction.

Closest City or Town: Cawker City

Address: 719 Wisconsin St., Cawker City, KS 67430

GPS Coordinates: 39.50991° N, 98.43360° W

Did You Know? In 1978, the record set by Frank in 1973 was broken by a bigger ball of twine in Minnesota. In 1982, Cawker City defended Frank's legacy by holding a Twine Ball Days festival to allow people to add twine to Frank's ball. Now, the ball contains almost 1,600 miles of twine.

Cheney State Park

Created in 1965, Cheney State Park features 1,913 acres of park area and 9,600 surface acres of water across three Kansas counties. It is a popular park for camping, fishing, and hiking, with 223 full-hookup RV sites, 400 primitive camp sites, six boat ramps, twenty-two launching lanes, four courtesy docks, four designated swimming areas, three nature trails, and plenty of shelters for picnics and group gatherings. The reservoir is stocked with a variety of fish species, including white bass, walleye, crappie, channel catfish, blue catfish, and white perch, among others. With the naturally windy conditions in central Kansas, Cheney Reservoir is an ideal place for sailing. The park is the location of several National Sailing regattas, where you'll see over 100 colorful sailboats on the water at a single time. Adjacent to the state park is the 5,200-acre Cheney Wildlife Area, which was established for migratory waterfowl and is only open between March 15 and September 15.

Best Time to Visit: The best time to visit is in the summer, especially for water activities and wildlife viewing.

Pass/Permit/Fees: There is a $5 fee per vehicle, per day to visit Cheney State Park.

Closest City or Town: Cheney

Address: 16000 NE 50 St, Cheney, KS 67025

GPS Coordinates: 37.72146° N, 97.83395° W

Did You Know? The Cheney State Park Trail is 9.6 miles long and features a mixture of forest and prairie landscapes, complete with wildflowers and grasses.

The Honking Tree

If ever there was a lucky tree, the Honking Tree would be it. The Honking Tree is a 100-year-old cottonwood that is still standing despite all odds. By the time a cottonwood gets to be this age, it's usually dying, and that's if it reaches that age at all. Many of them fall during high winds or heavy storms. Since Kanas is well known for tornados and other severe weather, the Honking Tree, which stands isolated along the road in an otherwise treeless landscape, is surprisingly still alive and standing tall. This tree has been called numerous names throughout the years, but recently it has been known as the "Honking Tree" because people honk as they pass by it in either direction for good luck. There are also many ribbons, memorials, and other mementos near the tree if you decide to stop and get a closer look.

Best Time to Visit: The best time to visit the Honking Tree is during the summer when it has leaves on its branches.

Pass/Permit/Fees: There is no fee to visit this attraction.

Closest City or Town: Colwich

Address: KS-96, Colwich, KS 67030

GPS Coordinates: 37.81902° N, 97.50969° W

Did You Know? In the 1990s, the Honking Tree was slated to be cut down to make way for an expansion to KS-96, but locals petitioned the Kansas Department of Transportation to save it. The engineers were able to route the expansion to the north of the tree and keep the monument in place.

Chase State Fishing Lake

This lake is considered one of the best places for fishing in Kansas because it was specifically designed as a fishing lake. There are eight fishing piers located around it, but you can also fish from rocks or the shore. Anglers appreciate the abundant stock of black bass, crappie, channel catfish, saugeye, white bass, and bluegill. You won't find a more diverse fishing population anywhere in the state.

A vast grass prairie surrounds the lake, and it's filled with various wildflowers that make for excellent photographs. Below the dam, there are several woody draws for hunting, which is allowed, but game population in the area is fairly limited. You may find quail, white-tailed deer, squirrels, turkeys, prairie chickens, and waterfowl available for hunting, but make sure what you're targeting is in season.

Best Time to Visit: The best time to visit Chase State Fishing Lake is during the spring and summer.

Pass/Permit/Fees: There is no fee to visit this area.

Closest City or Town: Cottonwood Falls

Address: 1461 Lake Rd., Cottonwood Falls, KS 66845

GPS Coordinates: 38.36793° N, 96.58777° W

Did You Know? Be sure to explore the area behind the dam to view several spectacular waterfalls. You can also camp in designated areas on the north shore of the lake. These are available on a first-come, first-served basis.

Cottonwood Falls

Cottonwood Falls is located in Chase County. It was initially settled in 1854 by a Native American trader named Seth Hayes, who established a cattle ranch along the Cottonwood River near the mouth of Diamond Spring Creek. The area around the ranch became Chase County in 1859, two years before Kansas was admitted to the Union. The city grew up quickly, with the first post office appearing in 1858.

The Chase County Courthouse was built in 1873 and is now the oldest continuously used courthouse west of the Mississippi. This was when the Atchison, Topeka, and Santa Fe Railway was extended to the Cottonwood Falls area. Today, the city is a stop along the Flint Hills National Scenic Byway for both its historical significance in the state and the beauty of the area.

Best Time to Visit: The best time to visit Cottonwood Falls is during the spring or fall to avoid the heat of the summer.

Pass/Permit/Fees: There is no fee to visit this location.

Closest City or Town: Cottonwood Falls

Address: Cottonwood Falls, KS 66845

GPS Coordinates: 38.36956° N, 96.54756° W

Did You Know? Cottonwood Falls is a wonderful place to browse antique shops, art galleries, and independent boutiques.

Council Grove

Native American trader and early settler Seth Hays came to the area now known as Council Grove in 1847 to trade with the Kaw Native American Tribe. Hays, who was a great-grandson of Daniel Boone, frequented the Santa Fe Trail, which is now Main Street of Council Grove. Hays opened a restaurant in 1857, and the city was officially incorporated a year later. The Hays House, which was the name of Hays's restaurant, is still in operation and is thought to be the oldest continuously operating restaurant west of the Mississippi River. Fifteen sites located in Council Grove are on the National Register of Historic Places, one of which is the Post Office Oak, a tree where travelers would leave their mail to be picked up by a mail wagon going in the right direction.

Best Time to Visit: The best time to visit is during the spring and fall when the temperatures are mild.

Pass/Permit/Fees: There is no fee to visit this attraction.

Closest City or Town: Council Grove

Address: Council Grove, KS, 66846

GPS Coordinates: 38.66089° N, 96.48950° W

Did You Know? The Custer Elm, another location in Council Grove that is on the National Register of Historic Places, is a large elm tree under which General Custer slept with his troops during the Civil War. Prisoners of war in World War II were brought to Council Grove to solve a labor shortage and were interned at a camp in Council Grove.

Trail Days Café & Museum

Housed in the Rawlinson-Terwilliger home that once sat along the Santa Fe Trail, the Trail Days Café & Museum was born out of the necessity of preventing the home from being bulldozed in 1994. Shirley McClintock established a nonprofit organization dedicated to saving the house. After significant renovations, McClintock turned it into a museum and eatery that would transport guests back in time to when the house served as a gas station and motor camp for guests passing by on the Santa Fe Trail. The house was built in 1860 and 1861. It was first a home to the Abraham and Mary Rawlinson family, who eagerly awaited the freight wagons that would pass by their home, which was the last stop that freighters would pass when heading west out of Council Grove. William Riley Terwilliger and his wife Mary purchased the house in 1870 and lived there with their fifteen children. In 1927, the house was converted to a gas station.

Best Time to Visit: The café and museum are open daily from 11:00 a.m. to 8:00 p.m.

Pass/Permit/Fees: There is no fee to visit the Trail Days Café & Museum, but donations are appreciated.

Closest City or Town: Council Grove

Address: 803 W. Main St., Council Grove, KS 66846

GPS Coordinates: 38.65952° N, 96.49879° W

Did You Know? The Trail Days Café & Museum has earned numerous awards, including the "2020 Best of the West" by *True West Magazine*.

Boot Hill Museum

This unique museum that celebrates the Old West is located on the original site of Boot Hill Cemetery. The hands-on exhibits and activities bring you up close and personal with rugged cowboys and old-fashioned gunfights. As you pass through the front doors of the museum, you'll travel back in time to the dusty roads of the 1870s. You'll learn about life in the Queen of Cow Towns back when everything west of Missouri was considered a cow town. Visit a reproduction of a Western town, complete with a saloon, general store, and more. The museum holds more than 20,000 artifacts, including 200 original guns. In the summer, live entertainment is scheduled daily, and simulated gunfights occur several times a day, even in the off season.

Best Time to Visit: The museum is open Monday through Saturday from 9:00 a.m. to 5:00 p.m. and on Sunday from 1:00 p.m. to 5:00 p.m.

Pass/Permit/Fees: Adult admission is $18 per person. Children between the ages of 5 and 12 are $12 per person. Seniors are $16 each, and children ages 4 and under are free.

Closest City or Town: Dodge City

Address: 500 W. Wyatt Earp Blvd., Dodge City, KS 67801

GPS Coordinates: 37.75438° N, 100.02183° W

Did You Know? "Boot Hill" was a term for cemeteries that were used to bury gunslingers who "died with their boots on" or in a violent manner.

Famous Gunfighters Wax Museum

After visiting Boot Hill in Dodge City, take some time to check out the nearby Famous Gunfighters Wax Museum. Creator Larry Yost bought the wax figures from a traveling carnival in 1957 and decided to build a museum to display them on the second floor of Yost's photography studio. He continued to add more wax figures throughout the next few years until the museum was full. After Yost moved out of the lower floor of the building in 1982, the Kansas Teachers' Hall of Fame took over but kept the Famous Gunfighters Wax Museum as it was. Some gunfighters represented in the museum include Jesse James, Calamity Jane, Belle Starr, Norma the Barmaid, the Dalton Gang, Billy the Kid, Joaquin Murieta, and Clay Allison. You'll also see other figures of the time, such as Doc Holliday and Sitting Bull.

Best Time to Visit: The museum is open in the summer Monday through Saturday from 10:00 a.m. to 5:00 p.m. and Sunday from 1:00 p.m. to 5:00 p.m.

Pass/Permit/Fees: Admission is $8 per person.

Closest City or Town: Dodge City

Address: 603 5th Ave., Dodge City, KS 67801

GPS Coordinates: 37.75472° N, 100.02276° W

Did You Know? Other wax figures in the museum include Frankenstein, Dracula, John F. Kennedy, and Lyndon B. Johnson. There's no real reason for them being in the museum other than they were part of Yost's collection.

Elk River Hiking Trail

A finalist in the effort to name the Eight Wonders of Kansas, Elk River Hiking Trail is a 15-mile National Recreation Trail that passes through the Chautauqua Hills region of the state. Having achieved the title of the best hike in Kansas from *Backpacker Magazine*, the trail winds around a rocky ridge to the north of a lake and passes under rock canopies, through rock tunnels, and along rock walls.

There are rock steps that will take you up to the bluffs that overlook the lake and around boulders the size of cars. The hike is challenging at times and should be reserved for hikers with at least some skill. The path is rugged, rocky, and sometimes steep.

Occasionally, rock climbing may be necessary depending on the path you ultimately take. Overall, it is a scenic hike that includes a waterfall, small cave, and spectacular views.

Best Time to Visit: The best time to visit the Elk River Hiking Trail is in the spring when the water is running high.

Pass/Permit/Fees: There is no fee to visit this area.

Closest City or Town: Elk City

Address: 4825 Squaw Creek Rd., Independence, KS 67301

GPS Coordinates: 37.26870° N, 95.90097° W

Did You Know? Follow the blue paint blazes on the path to ensure you stay on the route.

Cimarron National Grassland

Located in Morton County, the Cimarron National Grassland is administered by the U.S. Forest Service, the Pike and San Isabel national forests, and the Comanche National Grassland. Encompassing 108,176 acres, this is the largest public land area in Kansas. It is bisected by the Cimarron River, but the terrain is mostly flat, with a slight downward slope to the east. In the Cimarron Valley, the bluffs rise as high as 100 feet above the prairie.

The Comanche Native American tribe once claimed the territory that is now the Cimarron National Grassland, and William Becknell became the first settler to use the alternate route of the Santa Fe Trail, which passed through it. The first ranch in the area was the Point of Rocks Ranch, established by the Beaty Brothers in 1879. Currently, the grassland is used for recreational activities like hiking, fishing, hunting, horseback riding, and camping.

Best Time to Visit: Visit Cimarron National Grassland during the mild weather of the spring, summer, or fall.

Pass/Permit/Fees: There is no fee to visit this area.

Closest City or Town: Elkhart

Address: 242 Highway 56 E, Elkhart, KS 67950

GPS Coordinates: 37.12482° N, 101.79361° W

Did You Know? In 1831, mountain man Jedediah Smith was killed by members of the Comanche Native American tribe in the grasslands.

Subterra Castle

In 1982, Ed and Dianna Peden purchased a home about 25 miles outside of Topeka. It wasn't just any home, though. It was an abandoned underground missile launch complex, and it became the first one to be converted into a livable house. Now, the Pedens run a business to help other people convert missile silos into their own homes.

When they first opened the silo door, which weighed 47 tons and was designed to withstand a nuclear explosion, they had to remove crumbled and melted sheetrock, along with 9 feet of water. They turned the missile bay into a shop, and the launch control center is now a new age living space. There is a large eat-in kitchen, a laundry room, bathrooms, and home offices. In the former diesel generator room, the Pedens created a drum circle room where the couple hosts various drumming events.

Best Time to Visit: Tours are by appointment only, so contact Ed and Dianna Peden at info@missilebases.com to request information on their next tour date.

Pass/Permit/Fees: There is no fee to visit this attraction.

Closest City or Town: Eskridge

Address: 15513 Missile Base Rd., Eskridge, KS 66423

GPS Coordinates: 38.97786° N, 96.04914° W

Did You Know? Ed Peden originally purchased the abandoned missile silo for $40,000 from the federal government, which paid $4 million to build the silo and equip it with a missile during the Cold War.

Fort Scott National Historic Site

Fort Scott was established in 1842 when Kansas was considered the far west. However, within a few years, the soldiers stationed at Fort Scott would become a major part of the events that would lead to the nation's growth and expansion. Disputes over slavery led to a series of conflicts known as "Bleeding Kansas." In fact, it's the only National Historic Site that was directly involved with the confrontations related to the Kansas–Nebraska Act of 1854, which allowed residents to determine if they would enter the Union as free or slave states.

People with opposing viewpoints on this issue flooded into Kansas in an attempt to sway the vote in their favor. Conflict erupted between these two factions, and violence and destruction became common in the region. By 1859, approximately sixty people had died throughout the Kansas Territory as people fought over the issue of slavery.

Best Time to Visit: Visit Fort Scott National Historic Site during spring or fall when the weather is cooler.

Pass/Permit/Fees: There is no fee to visit this attraction.

Closest City or Town: Fort Scott

Address: 199 Old Fort Blvd., Fort Scott, KS 66701

GPS Coordinates: 37.84381° N, 94.70472° W

Did You Know? Visitors are able to tour eleven historically accurate buildings with thirty furnished rooms that tell the story of life in the mid-1800s.

Giant Van Gogh Painting

The Giant Van Gogh Painting is the perfect definition of a roadside attraction. The huge reproduction of Van Gogh's *Three Sunflowers in a Vase* is visible from I-70 when driving through Goodland. This painting, which is part of the Big Easel Project that started in 1996, was one of Cameron Cross's 24 feet by 32 feet reproductions given to Altona, Canada, Emerald, Australia, and Goodland, Kansas.

While there are four other paintings planned, they have not been completed yet. The giant painting sits upon an 80-foot steel easel and offers some interesting photo opportunities up close. The painting of the sunflowers fits in perfectly with the surrounding sunflower fields.

Best Time to Visit: The best time to visit the Giant Van Gogh Painting is during the day so that you can fully appreciate the size and capture excellent photos. The painting is not lit at night.

Pass/Permit/Fees: There is no fee to visit this attraction.

Closest City or Town: Goodland

Address: 1998 Cherry Ave., Goodland, KS 67735

GPS Coordinates: 39.33878° N, 101.70468° W

Did You Know? The easel and painting weigh 45,000 pounds, and the supports for the easel are buried 35 feet into the ground. The painting is 768 square feet but is not the largest in the world by a long shot—the largest one is 400,000 square feet.

Cheyenne Bottoms Refuge

The Cheyenne Bottoms Refuge is a 60 square miles natural depression located north of the Arkansas River. It is the largest marsh in the interior of the United States, and the Ramsar Convention on Wetlands designated it as a Wetland of International Importance in 1988. The reason this area is considered so important is that it's the main shorebird migration point in the western hemisphere.

About 45 percent of the North American shorebird population visits the Cheyenne Bottoms Refuge during spring migration. In addition to birds, the area is a known refuge for deer, beavers, raccoons, muskrats, sliders, Western painted turtles, diamondback snakes, northern water snakes, and more.

Best Time to Visit: The best time to visit Cheyenne Bottoms Refuge is during the spring when the birds are migrating.

Pass/Permit/Fees: There is no fee to visit this attraction.

Closest City or Town: Great Bend

Address: 204 NE 60 Rd., Great Bend, KS 67530

GPS Coordinates: 38.46988° N, 98.64893° W

Did You Know? Get an expansive view of the entire Cheyenne Bottoms Wildlife Area from the overlook platform, which is located near the K-156 park entrance. There are at least 320 species of birds that have used Cheyenne Bottoms as a waypoint during migration.

The Big Well

The Big Well is the name of the World's Largest Hand-Dug Well, which is located in Greensburg. It's 32 feet wide and 109 feet deep. It was originally dug in 1887 and 1888 by workers who used picks, shovels, a pulley and rope, and a barrel to haul up dirt. In 1916, a staircase and lightener were added, but it wasn't open to tourists until 1939 when visitors would pay to descend to the depths of the well. Eventually, the World's Largest Pallasite Meteorite was brought to the facility to be an additional above-ground attraction. In the building constructed around the well, you'll also find displays that tell the story of The Big Well and the tornado that came through the area in 2007 that destroyed nearly everything except the well and the meteorite. Guests can still walk down to the bottom of The Big Well.

Best Time to Visit: The Big Well is open Monday through Saturday from 9:00 a.m. to 6:00 p.m. and on Sunday from 1:00 p.m. to 6:00 p.m.

Pass/Permit/Fees: Admission is $8 per person.

Closest City or Town: Greensburg

Address: 315 S. Sycamore St., Greensburg, KS 67054

GPS Coordinates: 37.60409° N, 99.29397° W

Did You Know? After the devastating tornado, Greensburg rebuilt itself as a "model green city" and now has the most LEED-certified buildings per capita in the world. The city took the opportunity to turn tragedy (eleven people died in the twister) into a blessing.

The John Milburn Davis Grave

As a wealthy farmer with no children in the early 1900s, the community hoped that John Milburn Davis would use his money to benefit the town when his wife died. After all, he would have no heirs. But instead of using his wealth to build a hospital, park, school, or even a swimming pool, he built a grave for his wife and himself.

Milburn started by placing 7.5-ton granite slabs over their graves, then added six granite pillars and life-size marble statues of how he believed they would have looked on their 50th anniversary. Then, he added two other marble statues of how they'd looked on their 10th anniversary.

Eventually, he added six life-size statues around the graves (only five of his wife), with only one carved in granite. He once said that the people in Kansas hated him and that it was his money, so he'd spend it the way he pleased.

Best Time to Visit: The best time to visit the John Milburn Davis Grave is during daylight hours in the spring or fall.

Pass/Permit/Fees: There is no fee to visit this site.

Closest City or Town: Hiawatha

Address: 606 E. Iowa St., Hiawatha, KS 66434

GPS Coordinates: 39.85048° N, 95.51600° W

Did You Know? Davis never told anyone how much he spent on the grave, which he called the Davis Memorial, but it is estimated to be between $60,000 to $1 million.

Kansas Cosmosphere and Space Center

Established in 1962, the Kansas Cosmosphere and Space Center is a planetarium located on the campus of Hutchinson Community College. Initially, as one of the first planetariums in the central United States, it consisted of little more than a few folding chairs and a used planetarium projector in the Poultry Building on the Kansas State Fairgrounds. But, in 1980, a new 35,000-square-foot facility with a state-of-the-art planetarium opened to the public. It featured not only one of the first IMAX Dome Theaters, but also three floors of exhibits and classroom space for school programs. Attractions now include the Hall of Space Museum and more.

Best Time to Visit: The center is open Sunday through Thursday from 9:00 a.m. to 5:00 p.m. and on Friday and Saturday from 9:00 a.m. to 7:00 p.m.

Pass/Permit/Fees: Adult admission, which includes access to all activities and the planetarium, is $26.50. Children between the ages of 4 and 12 are $17.50. Seniors ages 60 and older and military members are $23.50.

Closest City or Town: Hutchinson

Address: 1100 N. Plum St., Hutchinson, KS 67501

GPS Coordinates: 38.06603° N, 97.92150° W

Did You Know? The Cosmosphere was one of the Smithsonian Institution's first affiliates due to its longstanding relationship with the Smithsonian's National Air & Space Museum.

Strataca

Formerly known as the Kansas Underground Salt Museum, Strataca is an underground display of the Permian Wellington Formation, one of the largest salt mines in the world. The Hutchison Salt Company (formerly the Carey Salt Mine) still mines salt in the area, with the purest portion of salt buried 650 feet underground.

Salt was originally discovered near Hutchinson in 1887, and it became the first large salt discovery west of the Mississippi River. The Carey Salt Mine opened in 1923 and began bringing this mineral to the surface. Strataca opened to the public in 1999 to give visitors an inside look at the business of mining salt in the area.

Best Time to Visit: Strataca is open Tuesday through Saturday from 9:00 a.m. to 6:00 p.m., with the last tour leaving at 4:00 p.m. On Sunday, the museum is open between 1:00 p.m. and 6:00 p.m.

Pass/Permit/Fees: Adult admission is $21 per person. Children ages 4 through 12 are $14 per person, and seniors ages 60 and over are $19 per person.

Closest City or Town: Hutchinson

Address: 3650 E. Avenue G, Hutchinson, KS 67501

GPS Coordinates: 38.04422° N, 97.86788° W

Did You Know? Four tons of salt are mined every three minutes, and the salt has been underground for approximately 250 million years.

Waterfalls at the Geary County Lake

Formed by an outlet of the Geary State Fishing Lake, the waterfalls at the Geary County Lake are among the most picturesque in the state. Due to the convenient location just a short distance off the road, you can make this stop as long or as quick as you want. The 35-foot falls may not be the tallest you'll ever see, but they flow for a significant distance, making them an incredible sight. The top of the falls is easy to reach via a worn path from the road, but if you want to hike to the bottom of the falls, the path is steep and can be slippery. The descent is not well marked, and you may encounter mud, trees, and even snakes on your way down. Since the waterfalls are created from lake overflow, there are times when the flow will be only a trickle or not running at all.

Best Time to Visit: The best time to visit is during the spring after a significant rainfall.

Pass/Permit/Fees: There is no fee to visit the waterfalls.

Closest City or Town: Junction City

Address: 1628-1914 State Lake Rd, Junction City, KS 66441

GPS Coordinates: 38.91094° N, 96.86266° W

Did You Know? The trail to the waterfalls at the Geary County Lake is 0.7 miles out and back, so the walk is not far to the top of the falls. It is rated as easy and appropriate for hikers of all ages, abilities, and skill levels. The path to the base of the falls is rated as moderately challenging.

Horsethief Trail

Horsethief Trail is a 1.9-mile loop trail that is considered moderately challenging because of its narrow, rocky terrain. There are three water crossings that aren't too difficult but may be deep in places. For this reason, take care when hiking this trail, and watch any young children or inexperienced hikers carefully. There are two different trails you can take.

The orange trail is harder to hike, but the water crossings are easier. The blue trail is easier to hike, but the water crossings are deeper. Even though the trail is narrow, it is heavily used by mountain bikes, equestrians, and hikers. There is room on the sides of the trail to allow oncoming or faster traffic to pass by. Be sure to bring a camera to capture the scenic views of this unique prairie-meets-desert landscape.

Best Time to Visit: The best time to visit Horsethief Trail is during the spring or fall when the weather isn't too hot.

Pass/Permit/Fees: There is a $5 fee per person to visit Kanopolis State Park, where the trailhead is located.

Closest City or Town: Kanopolis

Address: 200 Horsethief Rd., Marquette, KS 67464

GPS Coordinates: 38.65837° N, 97.99492° W

Did You Know? There are numerous unnamed caves throughout Kanopolis State Park that are just a short distance off Horsethief Trail. Take the time to explore the caves and small streams to enhance your experience.

Kansas Speedway

In 2001, the inaugural race was held at the Kansas Speedway, two years after breaking ground on the project. This is a 2.37-mile road course, and the spectator stands sit on over 1,200 acres. The track hosts various races from groups like the NASCAR Cup Series, the NASCAR Xfinity Series, the Indy Racing League, and the NASCAR Camping World Truck Series.

When the idea for a speedway was conceived in 1996, both the Missouri and Kansas sides of Kansas City were considered, but eventually, the International Speedway Corporation chose the Kansas side because that state offered better funding options. The speedway was designed by HNTB, which also designed the Chicagoland Speedway.

Best Time to Visit: NASCAR events are held twice a year, so if you want to see a NASCAR race, you'll want to visit on one of those two weekends. Other races are held at various times throughout the year. Check the website for dates and times.

Pass/Permit/Fees: The fee to visit the Kansas Speedway will depend on your race and seat selections.

Closest City or Town: Kansas City

Address: 400 Speedway Blvd., Kansas City, Kansas

GPS Coordinates: 39.11185° N, 94.83477° W

Did You Know? Originally, the speedway's capacity was supposed to be 75,000, but it was increased to 82,000 due to overwhelming demand for tickets.

Legends Field

Home of the Kansas City Monarchs, an American Association Professional Baseball team, and the Kansas City NWSL, a National Women's Soccer League team, Legends Field is a multi-purpose field that seats 6,537 fans for baseball and 10,385 fans for soccer. The field was built between September 2002 and June 2003. In 2008, additional bleacher seating was added to the left field to increase the capacity for baseball games beyond the original 4,365 seats. The T-Bones baseball team originally played in the stadium, which was initially called the CommunityAmerica Credit Union Ballpark, but the naming rights contract was not renewed in 2017. The stadium was temporarily called T-Bones Stadium, but the city evicted the team in 2019 for nonpayment of rent and utilities. Eventually, the team was sold and renamed the Monarchs in 2021.

Best Time to Visit: The best time to visit is during baseball or soccer season.

Pass/Permit/Fees: The fee to visit Legends Field depends on game and seat selection.

Closest City or Town: Kansas City

Address: 1800 Village West Pkwy, Kansas City, KS 66111

GPS Coordinates: 39.12530° N, 94.83117° W

Did You Know? The furthest seat from the field at this stadium is just 50 feet away, making this an excellent stadium for baseball and soccer fans who want to be close to the action.

Sauer Castle

Designed by the famous architect Asa Beebe Cross and completed in 1873, the Sauer Castle is an ornate house constructed in the Italianate style located in Kansas City. It was the home of Anton Sauer, originally from Vienna, Austria, who moved to Kansas City following his wife's death in 1868. The mansion sat on the Shawnee Indian Trail, which was a section of the Santa Fe Trail. The Sauers lived in the mansion for five generations until Paul Berry purchased it in 1955. Rumors that the mansion is haunted began circulating as early as 1930, which led to trespassing and vandalism during Berry's tenure. In 1987, ownership changed hands again with the intent to develop it into a bed and breakfast. That dream never materialized, and it was sold to Carl Lopp, a great-great-grandson of Anton Sauer, in 1988.

Best Time to Visit: Since the castle can only be viewed from the road, it is available to visit any time.

Pass/Permit/Fees: There is no fee to visit this attraction.

Closest City or Town: Kansas City

Address: 935 Shawnee Rd, Kansas City, KS 66103

GPS Coordinates: 39.06935° N, 94.63319° W

Did You Know? One of Sauer's sons-in-law committed suicide in the house, leading to rumors that the mansion was haunted.

Fort Larned National Historic Site

Fort Larned National Historic Site is a preserved 1860s Army fort located on the Santa Fe Trail that has a tumultuous past from during the period of the Indian Wars. Since the Santa Fe Trail was one of the most important transportation routes that allowed commercial traffic to flow between Independence, Missouri and Santa Fe, New Mexico, the influx of people through the area after the U.S. acquired vast amounts of land in the southwest caused significant turmoil among the American Indians living there. This led to a rise in conflicts between westbound travelers and Native Americans in the area, which prompted the U.S. Army to build Fort Larned to protect travelers and maintain peace. There are sandstone buildings on the property that were built to shelter Army troops who were referred to as the "Guardians of the Santa Fe Trail."

Best Time to Visit: While the park is open year-round, the best time to visit is during the spring or fall to avoid the hot weather of the summer.

Pass/Permit/Fees: There is no fee to visit this attraction.

Closest City or Town: Larned

Address: 1767 KS-156, Larned, KS 67550

GPS Coordinates: 38.18421° N, 99.22136° W

Did You Know? Following the 1864 Chivington Massacre at Sand Creek in the Colorado Territory, the War Department prohibited travel beyond Fort Larned without an armed escort.

Castle Rock

This giant limestone pillar is a landmark in Gove County. Part of the Smoky Hills region of Kansas, Castle Rock provided the travelers on the Overland Trail a way to get their bearings on their way out west. The formation was created by wind and water erosion and received its name because it looks like a castle riding above the plains. The path to the rock is extremely rough since the castle is located on private range land, and the route is unmaintained. The road has ruts of up to 18 inches in depth, so drivers who travel to the rock must be extremely vigilant and use four-wheel-drive. Travelers often feel like they are the first ones to discover Castle Rock because it is usually uncrowded (and often you'll be the only one there). There's nothing else around for miles.

Best Time to Visit: The best time to visit Castle Rock is during the spring, summer, or fall when the weather is warm.

Pass/Permit/Fees: There is no fee to visit this area.

Closest City or Town: Larrabee

Address: Located in the Chalk Badlands, Castle Rock is a remote destination without a precise physical address. It is located in Larrabee, KS 67752.

GPS Coordinates: 38.86366° N, 100.16985° W

Did You Know? Be sure to get close enough to the rock to see the millions of tiny fossils imbedded in the formation.

Chalk Badlands

The Chalk Badlands, located near Quinter, are home to the Castle Rock limestone formation. This area includes a 1.5-mile hiking loop that takes visitors past vibrant wildflowers. This trail is rated as moderate but is good for all skill levels. The reason it isn't rated easier is that the trail can get rocky in places. The Chalk Badlands is the name of the ancient Western Interior Seaway seabed that was once covered by ocean water.

In the area, you'll come across numerous chalk outcrops that are comprised of calcite and coccolith microfossils that were left behind when the ocean receded during the Cretaceous Period. The chalk formations provide a stark contrast to the otherwise flat plains of Kansas, particularly in the western part of the state. The yellow and gray pillars also provide a scenic foreground for photographs of the plains beyond.

Best Time to Visit: The best time to visit is during the warmer temperatures of spring, summer, and fall.

Pass/Permit/Fees: There is no fee to visit this location.

Closest City or Town: Larrabee

Address: This is a remote area without a specific physical address. It can be found in Larrabee, KS 67752.

GPS Coordinates: 38.86526° N, 100.16968° W

Did You Know? The layer of rock that is exposed in the badlands is called Niobrara Chalk. It's the basis for the University of Kansas's "Rock chalk, Jayhawk" chant.

Bloomington Beach

On the shore of Clinton Lake, Bloomington Beach is a large, sandy swimming beach that is managed by the U.S. Army Corps of Engineers. Nestled in the middle of the Cedar Ridge, Hickory/Walnut, and Oak campgrounds, the beach has numerous amenities, including indoor and outdoor showers, a playground, four picnic shelters, four volleyball courts, and an accessible fishing dock.

Completed in 1980, Bloomington Beach on Clinton Lake was originally built for flood control. Since then, it has become a popular destination for recreational activities. Beachgoers love the clean water and wooded shoreline, and the 7,000-acre lake provides enough space for everyone who comes to enjoy their time near or in the water.

Best Time to Visit: The best time to visit Bloomington Beach is during the summer, particularly for water activities. The beach is only open between May and September.

Pass/Permit/Fees: If you're not camping in one of the three campgrounds, there is a $5 fee per vehicle to visit Bloomington Beach. There is a $2 fee per person for walk-in visitors.

Closest City or Town: Lawrence

Address: 700 N. 1190 Rd., Lawrence, KS 66047

GPS Coordinates: 38.91120° N, 95.36830° W

Did You Know? Swimming is allowed in Clinton Lake, but not within 100 yards of the boat ramp or fishing dock.

Clinton State Park

This state park, located near Lawrence, offers a variety of recreational amenities, including a swimming beach, a marina, 378 campground sites (196 sites with water and electricity hookups, and 173 primitive sites), 6 cabins, a 25-mile biking and hiking trail, a 5-mile trail for cross-country skiing, an archery range, a sand volleyball court, an 18-hole disc golf course, a mountain bike skills course, a 1-acre fishing pond for children, a 3-acre trout pond, a fish cleaning station, and two fish feeders. The lake offers a variety of fishing species. The 7,000-acre lake is a popular destination for both fishing and swimming, especially in the summer. You can also reserve one of six shelters and playgrounds for group get-togethers.

Best Time to Visit: Visit the park in the summer for water activities and during the spring or fall for onshore activities.

Pass/Permit/Fees: There is no fee to visit this attraction.

Closest City or Town: Lawrence

Address: 798 N. 1415 Rd., Lawrence, KS 66049

GPS Coordinates: 38.93759° N, 95.36402° W

Did You Know? A pair of bald eagles has returned annually since 1989 to the Deer Creek arm of Clinton Lake to nest among the highly protected bluffs and prairies around the lake. Other wildlife, such as bullfrogs, squirrels, foxes, bobcats, beaver, and coyotes, can be spotted year-round.

Free State Brewing Company

When the Free State Brewing Company opened in Lawrence in 1989, it became the first legal brewery in the state in more than 100 years. Kansas was at the forefront of Prohibition, becoming the first state to ban alcohol in 1881. After Prohibition was repealed in 1933, it still took the state fifteen years before it changed its own laws.

When founder Chuck Magerl began thinking about opening a brewery, Kansans couldn't even have a beer or glass of wine with dinner at a restaurant. They had to belong to a private club if they wanted an alcoholic beverage. Magerl decided the alcohol laws in Kansas had to change, and he spent significant time talking with legislators and explaining his vision for a local brewery, not large ones like in St. Louis, Missouri or Golden, Colorado. His efforts were successful, and the brewery opened in an abandoned bus depot in 1989.

Best Time to Visit: Brewery tours are offered at 2:00 p.m. on the second Saturday of each month.

Pass/Permit/Fees: There is no fee to tour this facility.

Closest City or Town: Lawrence

Address: 636 Massachusetts St., Lawrence, KS 66044

GPS Coordinates: 38.9741° N, 95.23574° W

Did You Know? Owner Chuck Magerl's grandfather spent time in prison at Leavenworth for illegally making alcohol during Prohibition. His passion for brewing was passed down to his grandson.

Grinter Sunflower Farms

While there are hundreds of sunflower fields in Kansas, most of them are located in western and central Kansas. Grinter Sunflower Farms, though, is located in eastern Kansas and has become the go-to place for photographs with sunflowers, especially for the larger cities of Topeka and Kansas City. In fact, professional photographers schedule sessions at the farms because of its pristine conditions.

Visitors need to be respectful of the property and surrounding farms, but they'll even be allowed to pick a sunflower to give to a special someone or keep for themselves. This is a seasonal operation, so you should follow the farm on social media to know when to visit. You can also enjoy tractor and combine rides and sweet corn picking during your visit.

Best Time to Visit: The farms are open to visitors from 9:00 a.m. to 5:00 p.m. during the season that the sunflowers are in bloom, which is in late August.

Pass/Permit/Fees: There is no fee to visit this attraction.

Closest City or Town: Lawrence

Address: 24154 Stillwell Rd., Lawrence, KS 66044

GPS Coordinates: 39.04760° N, -95.13946° W

Did You Know? In 2020, the Grinter family opened Sunflower General, a bakery and food shop that features local items. Visitors say the best delicious treat from here is a peanut butter chocolate chip cookie.

Potter Lake

In the early 20th century, the University of Kansas was in the middle of a constructing numerous buildings on top of Mount Oread, and they realized that if a fire occurred on the hill, there would be no way to extinguish it. The only water supply available then was a small City of Lawrence water line. The university decided to create a lake that could provide a supply of water for up to forty-eight hours in case a fire broke out. The project began in 1910 and was completed in 1911. A 400-foot dam was constructed to hold back 4 million gallons of water in the reservoir. Since then, the lake has become a popular location for University of Kansas students who are seeking a quiet place for reflection and study, or a frozen surface to skate on in the winter. It is also a favorite place for local fishermen, who can catch copious numbers of bass and crappie in the water.

Best Time to Visit: The best time to visit the lake is during the spring and summer for fishing and in the winter for ice skating.

Pass/Permit/Fees: There is no fee to visit the lake.

Closest City or Town: Lawrence

Address: 1450 Jayhawk Blvd., Lawrence, KS 66045-7594

GPS Coordinates: 38.96109° N, 95.24880° W

Did You Know? A month before the lake was opened to the public, a group of engineering students decided to swim across it. One member, Leonard Ritchey, didn't make it and died from heart failure.

Prairie Park Nature Center

This 100-acre nature preserve opened to the public in 1999 to provide educational opportunities to visitors. There is a 5-acre lake, woodlands, wetlands, and prairie habitat on the property. This area gives guests the opportunity to observe various native wildlife such as deer, beavers, bobcats, and birds of prey. There are several trails that are excellent for wildlife and birdwatching or for walking field trips for schools and other groups. Inside the education building, there are dioramas of natural habitats, live-animal displays, and other exhibits. Be sure to check out the live bird of prey collection that features falcons, eagles, hawks, and owls. Mary's Lake is open for public fishing and is stocked with channel catfish and bass throughout the spring and summer. A valid Kansas fishing license is required to fish at Mary's Lake.

Best Time to Visit: The best time to visit for fishing is in the spring and summer. For other activities, the spring and fall are best because the weather is cooler.

Pass/Permit/Fees: There is no fee to visit the center.

Closest City or Town: Lawrence

Address: 2730 Harper St., Lawrence, KS 66046

GPS Coordinates: 38.93337° N, 95.21664° W

Did You Know? Prairie Park Nature Center features a different animal each month, using rescued, rehabilitated wildlife to educate visitors on their lives and habitats. Past featured animals include ferrets, hawks, owls, and more.

Spencer Museum of Art

The Spencer Museum of Art began in 1917 with the donated collection of 7,500 pieces of art from Sallie Casey Thayer to the University of Kansas. Her goal was to "Encourage the study of fine arts in the Middle West." She had an expansive collection of sculptures, paintings, drawings, furniture, prints, rugs, metalwork, glass, ceramics, textiles, and more. They were primarily obtained in Asia and Europe and were rare to see on the U.S. side of the ocean. In 1928, the University of Kansas Museum of Art was established and continued to grow throughout the intervening years. In 2007, the museum was renamed the Spencer Museum of Art when it expanded to include the 8,500 ethnographic objects from the former University of Kansas Museum of Anthropology. The new collection included numerous cultural objects related to Native American history.

Best Time to Visit: The museum is open Tuesday through Friday from 10:00 a.m. to 5:00 p.m. For a less crowded experience, visit when school is not in session.

Pass/Permit/Fees: There is no fee to visit the museum.

Closest City or Town: Lawrence

Address: 1301 Mississippi St., Lawrence, KS 66045

GPS Coordinates: 38.96026° N, 95.24444° W

Did You Know? The Spencer Museum of Art now has a collection of more than 45,000 objects that span European and American art history from ancient times to contemporary art. It has a special focus on East Asian art.

The Granada Theater

Originally built in 1928 as a Vaudeville theater, the Granada underwent renovation in 1934 to show silent films. The first movie shown at the theater was the 1934 comedy *Hide-Out*, starring Robert Montgomery and Maureen O'Sullivan. After temporarily closing in 1989, the theater was renovated a second time in 1993 to become a live music and comedy venue.

The theater has hosted such acts as M83, Weezer, Flaming Lips, Pat Green, Jerry Cantrell, John Mayer, Marilyn Manson, Big Head Todd, The Roots, Smashing Pumpkins, Creek, Henry Rollins, Blink 182, and others. The Kansas City-based band The Get Up Kids recorded a live album at the theater in 2005. The theater can be rented out for private events such as holiday parties, fundraisers, fashion shows, and receptions.

Best Time to Visit: The best time to visit is when there is a concert scheduled that you want to see. Check the website for showtimes and dates.

Pass/Permit/Fees: The fee to visit the theater depends on show and seat selection.

Closest City or Town: Lawrence

Address: 1020 Massachusetts St., Lawrence, KS 66044

GPS Coordinates: 38.96561° N, 95.23573° W

Did You Know? The Granada Theater originally had a capacity of 2,300 people, but it currently only seats 900.

Watkins Museum of History

Located in the historic 1888 Watkins Land Mortgage and National Bank Building, the Watkins Museum of History has been providing the community with educational opportunities, cultural experiences, and evolving exhibits that display the history of Douglas County since 1975. Included in the permanent exhibits is information about two of Lawrence's most famous residents: Dr. John Naismith (inventor of basketball and a University of Kansas coach) and Langston Hughes (poet, playwright, novelist, and columnist). The museum is also home to a large genealogy project that contains research resources such as marriage, death, and land records, family history documents, photographs, maps, telephone directories, immigration and early history files, and local church history. The building in which the museum is housed was considered one of the most stunning examples of Richardsonian Romanesque architecture west of the Mississippi.

Best Time to Visit: The museum is open Tuesday through Saturday from 10:00 a.m. to 4:00 p.m.

Pass/Permit/Fees: There is no fee to visit this attraction.

Closest City or Town: Lawrence

Address: 1047 Massachusetts St., Lawrence, KS 66044

GPS Coordinates: 38.96463° N, 95.23614° W

Did You Know? Must-see artifacts in the museum include James Naismith's desk, the "Old Sacramento" cannon, John Brown's pike, and the Eldridge chair.

Weaver's Department Store

As the longest continuously operating department store west of the Mississippi River, Weaver's Department Store has been serving the Lawrence community since 1857, years before the University of Kansas was established in the city in 1865. The 20,000-square-foot store has just about anything you could ever want throughout its four floors.

Originally, Weaver's was a dry goods store owned and operated by Lathrop Bullene, but it was purchased by A. D. Weaver in 1886. Despite the threats of chain stores like Sears, JCPenney, and Woolworths, Weaver's was able to weather the challenges to be one of the last remaining independent department stores in the region.

Best Time to Visit: Weaver's is open Monday through Saturday from 10:00 a.m. to 6:00 p.m. and Sunday from 11:00 a.m. to 4:00 p.m.

Pass/Permit/Fees: There is no fee to visit the store, but you may want to bring money to shop.

Closest City or Town: Lawrence

Address: 901 Massachusetts St., Lawrence, KS 66044

GPS Coordinates: 38.96810° N, 95.23633° W

Did You Know? Weaver's Department Store opened as a dry goods store a year before R. H. Macy opened his "fancy dry goods" store in New York, which would eventually become Macy's.

Geographical Center of the Lower 48 States

The geographical center of the lower 48 states is located near Lebanon, Kansas and is marked by a 7-foot-high monument topped with a U.S. flag and a Kansas flag. There is also a bronze plate on the monument that indicates it was built by the Lebanon Hub Club on April 25, 1940.

The monument is surrounded mostly by fields, which is appropriate since much of Kansas is covered in fields. While there is some controversy that this is the exact center of the U.S.—Rand-McNally once stated that the center was actually in Nebraska—the U.S. Geological Survey said that Lebanon would be "the point where a plane map of the 48 states would balance if it were of uniform thickness."

Best Time to Visit: The best time to visit is during daylight hours.

Pass/Permit/Fees: There is no fee to visit this location.

Closest City or Town: Lebanon

Address: There is not a precise address, so using coordinates will help. Take Kansas State Highway 191 W in Lebanon, KS 66952.

GPS Coordinates: 39.82930° N, 98.57931° W

Did You Know? Recently, there has been consensus that this monument does represent the center of the lower forty-eight states, but the actual middle point is about 2,270 feet northwest of the monument.

Chalk Pyramids

The Chalk Pyramids, also referred to as Monument Rocks National Natural Landmark, is located near Oakley. The rock outcroppings are 70 feet tall and consist of Niobrara Chalk. They were formed by the erosion of an ancient seabed from the Western Interior Seaway that formed about 80 million years ago during the Cretaceous Period.

The Chalk Pyramids are relatively soft, so they change shape from year to year. They are on private land, but the owners allow visitors to stop by and check out the incredible structures. The Monument Rocks Natural Area was designated as a National Natural Landmark in 1968 by the U.S. Department of the Interior.

Best Time to Visit: The owners of the private land upon which the pyramids are situated only allow visitors during daylight hours.

Pass/Permit/Fees: There is no fee to visit this area.

Closest City or Town: Lewis

Address: The Chalk Pyramids are remote and do not have a physical address. You can find them in Lewis, KS 67748, using GPS coordinates.

GPS Coordinates: 38.79915° N, 100.76489

Did You Know? The Kansas Sampler Foundation chose Monument Rocks as one of the Eight Wonders of Kansas in 2007. Be sure to look for shells and other fossils in bands of sediment in the rocks. These are aquatic creatures that got caught in the limestone when the sea receded.

Coronado Heights Castle

In the 1540s, Spanish explorer Francisco Vasquez de Coronado is rumored to have visited the middle of what is now Kansas looking for the mythical "Seven Cities of Cibola." Legend had it that these cities were sites of wealth that lured explorers to endlessly hunt for them. Coronado set out to find the cities beginning in 1539 and traveled more than 4,000 miles in his search. He never found them, of course, but he didn't want to admit defeat, so he returned to Spain claiming to have found one.

However, he said it was nowhere nearly as rich as the legend had stated. A mysterious Spanish coin found in 1881 in Lindsborg gave rise to the idea that this was the city Coronado had found. In the 1930s, the 300-foot-high stone castle that stands in the area now was built to mark the spot where it is believed Coronado traveled on his quest.

Best Time to Visit: The best time to visit Coronado Heights Castle is during the spring, summer, and fall.

Pass/Permit/Fees: There is no fee to visit this attraction.

Closest City or Town: Lindsborg

Address: Smoky View, KS 67442

GPS Coordinates: 38.61428° N, 97.70312° W

Did You Know? Other activities you can do while at Coronado Heights Castle include picnicking, hiking, and biking. There's a three-mile trail around the castle.

Grassroots Art Center

The eclectic Garden of Eden isn't the only oddball art you'll find in Lucas, Kansas. The Grassroots Art Center was inspired by the "outsider art" produced by Sam Dinsmoor and contains artwork that may never find its way to a traditional museum. For instance, there are faces made from used chewing gum, a full-size car made from aluminum can pull tabs, rock sculptures, Barbie doll scenes, limestone carvings, mixed media collages, a concrete rock garden, wood carvings, barbed wire art, metal totem poles, wire sculptures, grapefruit rind sculptures, bottle art, scrap wood sculptures, and much more. Many of the artists are older, self-taught individuals who have taken up their craft during retirement. They are usually driven by a vision that takes the form of their art.

Best Time to Visit: The center is open in the summer Monday through Saturday from 10:00 a.m. to 5:00 p.m. and Sunday from 1:00 p.m. to 5:00 p.m.

Pass/Permit/Fees: Admission is $7 per person.

Closest City or Town: Lucas

Address: 213 S. Main St., Lucas, KS 67648

GPS Coordinates: 39.05804° N, 98.53859° W

Did You Know? The Grassroot Arts Center is located in three buildings in downtown Lucas, but work from its artists can be seen throughout town, including Bowl Plaza, a toilet-shaped restroom located a few blocks from the main galleries.

The Garden of Eden

As a finalist of the Eight Wonders of Kansas, The Garden of Eden is a world-famous grassroots art site that is home to one of the most intriguing sculpture gardens in the world. Civil War veteran Samuel Perry Dinsmoor, at the age of sixty-two in 1907, created the first sculpture when he used limestone logs to build his family home. He then took 113 tons of cement and constructed 40-foot trees to contain his giant sculpture garden. Every structure on the property has a secret meaning about politics, the Bible, and modern civilization. They eventually tell a complete story about Dinsmoor's eccentric worldview. The locals attempted to run Dinsmoor out of town numerous times while he was building his odd garden, but today, it's the town's main attraction.

Best Time to Visit: The Garden of Eden is open daily from May through October during the hours of 10:00 a.m. to 5:00 p.m. In November through February, it is only open on Saturday and Sunday from 1:00 p.m. to 4:00 p.m.

Pass/Permit/Fees: Adult admission is $6. Children between the ages of 6 and 12 are $1, and children ages 5 and under are free.

Closest City or Town: Lucas

Address: 305 E 2nd St, Lucas, KS 67648

GPS Coordinates: 39.05867° N, 98.53512° N

Did You Know? In 1927, at the age of eighty-four, Dinsmore stopped working on the garden because he went blind.

World's Largest Collection of Smallest Versions of Largest Things Museum

This museum not only has one of the longest names of any museum in the United States, but it's also one of the most entertaining. Owner Erika Nelson travels the country on a search for the world's largest things. Then, she makes the world's smallest version of that world's largest thing. If that sounds confusing, it's actually very simple. For example, take the world's largest ball of twine, which is located in Cawker. Nelson traveled to that location, took a photograph of the item, then returned to Lucas to create the smallest ball of twine. When possible, she returns to the original location with the smallest item to take a picture of the largest and smallest items together. This eclectic art museum is a fun side attraction that you'll talk about for years.

Best Time to Visit: Since Nelson is both the owner and operator of the museum, it may or may not be open when you arrive. It's best to call the museum directly at 785-760-0826 and make an appointment to see the art.

Pass/Permit/Fees: There is no fee to visit this museum.

Closest City or Town: Lucas

Address: 214 S. Main St., Lucas, KS 67648

GPS Coordinates: 39.05845° N, 98.53796° W

Did You Know? The museum began as a traveling exhibition in a bus with the miniatures displayed in the windows. It now has a storefront location.

Johnny Kaw Statue

Johnny Kaw is an American folklore character created by George Filinger, a horticulture professor at Kansas State University. In 1955, Filinger was annoyed that the state's newspapers were ignoring the city of Manhattan's 100th birthday. He decided that a larger-than-life character who represented the state would inspire pride in Kansas history. Johnny Kaw was bigger than Paul Bunyan and the color of Kansas wheat. He could make it rain by cutting into tornados with his scythe. He and Pecos Bill dug the Grand Canyon, and Johnny used the dirt to make Kansas flat for farming. When Paul Bunyan trampled Johnny's fields, he plowed the Mississippi Riverbed with Bunyan's face. In light of this character's incredible prowess, the town decided to erect a statue. While it took 11 years to raise the funds for Johnny's statue, the town didn't skimp on materials. Built out of concrete and steel, the statue survived a tornado just a month after its dedication without even a scratch.

Best Time to Visit: The best time to visit the Johnny Kaw Statue is in daylight hours.

Pass/Permit/Fees: There is no fee to visit this attraction.

Closest City or Town: Manhattan

Address: N. 11th St, Manhattan, KS

GPS Coordinates: 39.18306° N, 96.57368° W

Did You Know? The Johnny Kaw Statue was purposely built to stand taller than the 26-foot-tall Paul Bunyan statue in Brainerd, Minnesota.

Konza Prairie Biological Station

This native tallgrass prairie is jointly owned by Kansas State University and The Nature Conservancy. It's located in the Flint Hills area. The main function of Konza Prairie Biological Station is to provide a field research station for the KSU Division of Biology, which is committed to long-term ecological research, prairie conservation, and education. In this outdoor laboratory, scientists can study the tallgrass prairie ecosystem and conduct biological research on various natural processes. Since it was established in 1971, more than 1,680 scientific papers have been published out of the work conducted at Konza Prairie Biological Station, and more than 260 graduate students have been awarded their master's or PhD degrees based on their Konza Prairie Biological Station research.

Best Time to Visit: Visit Konza Prairie Biological Station during the spring or fall when the weather is cooler.

Pass/Permit/Fees: There is no fee to visit this attraction.

Closest City or Town: Manhattan

Address: 100 Konza Prairie Ln., Manhattan, KS 66502

GPS Coordinates: 39.10703° N, 96.60912° W

Did You Know? While most of the facility is on private land and closed to the public, the Konza Prairie Nature Trail and other hiking trails are open for visitors to learn about the endangered tallgrass ecosystem. Be sure to follow the posted rules to protect the wildlife, landscape, and ecological importance of the site.

Pillsbury Crossing Wildlife Area

The Pillsbury Crossing Wildlife Area is a popular location for hikers, fishermen, canoeists, and kayakers. Many people also come to visit the scenic 5-foot Deep Creek Waterfall. The area is named for a low-water river crossing that vehicles must pass when driving to the falls on Pillsbury Crossing Lane. There is an approximately 100-foot stretch of road that is covered by a few inches of water. Deep Creek Waterfall is just a few feet from the river and can be reached by a short hike from the parking spaces on the east side of Pillsbury Crossing Wildlife Area. You can also reach the waterfall from the north side, but you will need to descend a 30-foot rock face. It isn't a difficult descent, but the rocks can be extremely slippery when they get wet, which will happen since you have to walk through shallow water on the way down.

Best Time to Visit: The best time to visit is in the spring when the river and waterfall are running at their highest levels.

Pass/Permit/Fees: There is no fee to visit the area.

Closest City or Town: Manhattan

Address: 2464–2484 Pillsbury Crossing Ln., Manhattan, KS 66502

GPS Coordinates: 39.13211° N, 96.44131° W

Did You Know? The 59-acre area was donated to the Department of Wildlife and Parks in 1967. It is named for pioneer J. H. Pillsbury, who settled in the area in 1855.

Tuttle Creek State Park

This 1,200-acre park offers several nature trails, a scenic equestrian trail, and a mountain-biking trail to allow visitors to explore the gorgeous Flint Hills. Other amenities in the park include an 18-hole disc-golf course, horseshoe pits, and volleyball courts. The Fancy Creek Shooting Range, a state-of-the-art shooting facility, is open the first and third weekends each month, and the Luke Nihart archery range, located at the River Pond Area, is open during daylight hours. The 10,900-acre Tuttle Creek Lake is a prime spot for fishing, and it's stocked with various fish, including channel catfish, flathead, saugeye, white bass, largemouth bass, crappie, and trout. Wildlife that may be seen in the park include shorebirds, waterfowl, white-tailed deer, turkeys, quail, squirrels, doves, and pheasants.

Best Time to Visit: The best time to visit is during the spring and fall when the weather is cooler.

Pass/Permit/Fees: There is a $5 fee per vehicle to visit the park.

Closest City or Town: Manhattan

Address: 5800 River Pond Rd A, Manhattan, KS 66502

GPS Coordinates: 39.27237° N, 96.57992° W

Did You Know? Tuttle Creek Lake is the second-largest lake in Kansas, making it an excellent option for water recreation. Boating, camping, and swimming (in the River Pond Area) are all popular activities at this state park.

Kanopolis Lake State Park

Kanopolis Lake State Park has the distinction of being the first state park in Kansas. Its rolling hills, scenic woodlands, and Dakota-sandstone bluffs make it an ideal place to spend a day in nature. More than 30 miles of trails are open to mountain bikers, hikers, and horseback riders throughout the park. Fifteen of these trails pass through the Smoky Hill Wildlife Area. The 3,500-acre lake provides excellent fishing opportunities for anglers, where they can fish for crappie, trout, channel catfish, saugeye, wiper, and white bass. Hunting in the park is also a popular activity, with abundant wildlife available to track. The Faris Caves, located in the northwest part of the Smoky Hill Wildlife Area, give visitors a glimpse of early pioneer life, as the structures were carved by these settlers to serve as their milk house, living quarters, and schoolhouse.

Best Time to Visit: The best time to visit Kanopolis Lake State Park is during hunting season or in the spring or fall to avoid the heat of summer.

Pass/Permit/Fees: There is a $5 fee per vehicle to visit.

Closest City or Town: Marquette

Address: 200 Horsethief Rd., Marquette, KS 67464

GPS Coordinates: 38.71063° N, 98.10091° W

Did You Know? Wildlife viewing and photography are favorite activities of visitors to Kanopolis State Park, with opportunities to spot bald eagles, pheasants, prairie chickens, prairie dogs, and coyotes, among others.

McPherson Opera House

The McPherson Opera House opened in 1889 and has served as a cultural center for the community, providing a space for live performances, suffrage meetings, political rallies, movies, and more. Following a major $8.5 million renovation in the 1990s and 2000s that saved the building from destruction, the McPherson Opera House now provides modern facilities such as an art center, a premiere performance area, and meeting rooms. The building's architecture has been cited as a showpiece for opera house structures in Kansas, with its molded brick trim, limestone arches and cornices, and double balconies. Originally designed to seat 900 patrons, the opera house provides an intimate setting for live artistic performances.

Best Time to Visit: Self-guided tours of the McPherson Opera House are available Monday through Friday from 9:30 a.m. to 4:30 p.m. Guided tours are available by appointment only. If you want to attend a performance, check the website for showtimes and dates.

Pass/Permit/Fees: Self-guided tours are $5 per person. Guided tours are $9 per person.

Closest City or Town: McPherson

Address: 219 S. Main St. #4843, McPherson, KS 67460

GPS Coordinates: 38.36814° N, 97.66679° W

Did You Know? In the 1950s, the Mac Theater at McPherson Opera House showed double feature films, cartoons, and a serial for young children and teens. It eventually went dark in 1965 with the advent of television.

Gypsum Hills

Gypsum Hills is a scenic byway in Kansas that is 42 miles long. It starts at the western border of Medicine Lodge and ends at the intersection of US-160 and US-183 in Coldwater. It passes through the Gypsum Hills, which are noted for scenic views of wildflowers, high plains, red soil, and green cedar trees. At the beginning of the scenic drive in Medicine Lodge, and along the route, there are several recreational opportunities throughout the year that include fishing, swimming, boating, hunting, hiking, trail riding, birdwatching, backpacking, and spelunking. Additionally, you're almost sure to see wildlife throughout the drive, including deer, quail, turkeys, pheasants, skunks, beavers, raccoons, bobcats, armadillos, and porcupines.

Best Time to Visit: The best time to visit Gypsum Hills is during the spring and summer when the wildflowers are in bloom.

Pass/Permit/Fees: There is no fee to visit this attraction.

Closest City or Town: Medicine Lodge

Address: US-160, Medicine Lodge, KS 67104

GPS Coordinates: 37.40961° N, 98.62946° W

Did You Know? The Gypsum Hills are also known as the Red Hills, Gyp Hills, and Medicine Hills. The area was a prominent home for Native Americans due to the proximity to the Medicine River and abundant vegetation. There are also over 100 caves and several collapsed natural bridges along the route.

The Carrie Nation Home

The Carrie Nation Home was the home of Carrie A. Nation, a passionate temperance movement leader who lived in Medicine Lodge from 1889 to 1902. According to Nation's own words, in 1899, she received a vision from heaven to travel to Kiowa and destroy three saloons with a hatchet in her bid to prevent people from consuming alcohol. In 1902, Nation sold her house and used the proceeds to establish a home in Kansas City to house the wives of drunkards. In the 1950s, the Women's Christian Temperance Union purchased the house and preserved it as a museum.

Best Time to Visit:
Between June and October, the home is open Monday through Saturday from 10:30 a.m. to 5:00 p.m. and Sunday from 1:00 p.m. to 5:00 p.m. Between November and May, it is open daily from 1:00 p.m. to 4:00 p.m.

Pass/Permit/Fees:
Adult admission is $5 per person, and children between the ages of 7 and 14 are $3. Seniors ages 55 and older are $4.

Closest City or Town:
Medicine Lodge

Address: 211 W Fowler Ave, Medicine Lodge, KS 67104

GPS Coordinates: 37.27635° N, 98.58230° W

Did You Know? Admission includes entrance to the adjacent Stockade Museum, which once housed settlers and protected them against Native American attacks.

Rock City

Rock City is a 5-acre park that features approximately 200 giant Dakota-sandstone formations. The largest rock in the park is 27 feet in diameter, and some formations are as tall as 15 feet. Guests are encouraged to climb on them and explore the park. There is no other place in the world with as many sandstone rock formations like the ones in the park, and it was designated a natural landmark in 1978 by the U.S. Heritage Conservation and Recreation Service.

One of the most unique rocks in the park is Donut Hole Rock, which, as you might guess, looks like a donut on its edge. Another rock that provides an excellent photographic background is The Shipwreck, which resembles a sinking ship. Visitors have been coming to the area for picnics and gatherings since at least 1900.

Best Time to Visit: The best time to visit Rock City is in the spring or fall when the weather is cooler.

Pass/Permit/Fees: There is a suggested donation of $3 for adults and $0.50 for children.

Closest City or Town: Minneapolis

Address: 1051 Ivy Rd., Minneapolis, KS 67467

GPS Coordinates: 39.09151° N, 97.73542° W

Did You Know? The rocks in the park are known as calcite-cemented concretions or "cannonball concretions." They are formed by medium-grained sandstone tightly cemented by calcite. They formed when the calcite diffused through sandstone that was once deeply buried.

Little Jerusalem Badlands State Park

While there are many Niobrara Chalk formations in the western part of Kansas, the ones at Little Jerusalem Badlands State Park are the most dramatic. Not only do they strike a stark contrast with the flat prairies for which the state is known, but they also provide important habitats for various plants and animals.

Numerous reptiles, amphibians, and birds call Little Jerusalem home, and it is also where you'll find the largest population of Great Plains wild buckwheat, a native plant that grows only in the chalk bluffs prairie of western Kansas. The name "Little Jerusalem" is derived from the way the chalk formations resemble the ancient walled city of Jerusalem from a distance. Other incredible chalk formations in the area are on private land, but Little Jerusalem is a public park that everyone can enjoy.

Best Time to Visit: Visit during the spring or fall when the weather is cooler.

Pass/Permit/Fees: There is a $5 fee per vehicle to visit Little Jerusalem Badlands State Park.

Closest City or Town: Oakley

Address: County Rd. 400 and Gold Rd., Oakley, KS 67748

GPS Coordinates: 38.80320° N, 100.92878° W

Did You Know? Take the Life on the Rocks Trail to overlook the park from two scenic stops along the way. The Overlook Trail also provides a spectacular view from its crushed rock viewpoint.

Smoky Valley Ranch

This working cattle ranch is also home to several flourishing wildlife populations, such as a bison herd, lesser-prairie chickens, and pronghorns. These sights are some of the rarest in the U.S. since many of these animals are no longer allowed to roam freely throughout the country. Smoky Valley Ranch was purchased by The Nature Conservancy in 1999, and the 18,000 acres became the largest conservation area in Kansas.

This conservation area is important because 80 percent of western Kansas prairie land has been converted for other purposes. This ranch supports various wildlife and plants while continuing to operate as a cattle ranch. It's dedicated to making sure that the remaining 20 percent of the prairie that's left is protected and maintained. The lesser-prairie chicken relies on this prairie for its survival, and the ranch provides specific grassland grazing strategies that encourage the nesting and brooding of this species.

Best Time to Visit: The best time to visit the Smoky Valley Ranch is during the spring or fall for cooler weather.

Pass/Permit/Fees: There is no fee to visit this attraction.

Closest City or Town: Oakley

Address: 1114 County Rd. 370, Oakley, KS 67748

GPS Coordinates: 38.89030° N, 101.01923° W

Did You Know? Much of the land on the Smoky Valley Ranch is leased to local farmers for cattle grazing.

Heritage Park

Maintained by the Johnson County Park & Recreation District, Heritage Park is a 1,238-acre park that features a 40-acre lake, a 30-acre dog park, ten picnic shelters, playgrounds, outdoor exercise equipment, an 18-hole disc golf course, an 18-hole championship golf course, a driving range, soccer fields, and football fields. It is truly a recreational area with something for everyone.

Visitors can fish and boat on the lake, but a state fishing license is required. The dog park is one of the nicest in the state, with a fenced open area, a looped trail, and a small pond. Tall shade trees and a large play area make the dog park a joy for all pooches. The golf course is a fun and interesting design, with water features, varying terrain, Bentgrass greens, and Zoysia grass fairways.

Best Time to Visit: The best time to visit Heritage Park is during the spring, summer, or fall, especially for water activities and golf.

Pass/Permit/Fees: There is no fee to visit this attraction.

Closest City or Town: Olathe

Address: 16050 S. Pflumm Rd, Olathe, KS 66062

GPS Coordinates: 38.83842° N, 94.74281° W

Did You Know? Anglers love Heritage Lake for its abundant stock of channel catfish, bluegill, and largemouth bass. It is also considered a great place to teach children to fish since you're able to fish from the shore or a boat.

Lake Olathe Park

This 258-acre community park and 170-acre lake is full of recreational activities for visitors. The lake is a popular location for boating, fishing, kayaking, and paddle boarding. The swimming beach is a favorite place to relax when out of the water. The beach features amenities such as outdoor showers, a floating obstacle course, locker rooms, vending machines, lifeguards, and an early hours splash time that can be reserved for groups and parties. A marina, spray ground, nature playground, disc-golf course, fishing pavilion, covered shelters, and outdoor deck known as Eagles Landing round out the modern amenities at this park. There is also an amphitheater with ample seating for 1,500 visitors, where community events are often held.

Best Time to Visit: The best time to visit Lake Olathe Park is during the summer, especially for water activities.

Pass/Permit/Fees: The fee to visit depends on the activity you want to do. Contact the park directly for individual activity rates.

Closest City or Town: Olathe

Address: 625 S. Lakeshore Dr., Olathe, KS 66061

GPS Coordinates: 38.87369° N, 94.87346° W

Did You Know? Be sure to check out the interactive musical art sculptures located throughout the park. There are seven sculptures created by artist Po Shu Wang to replicate the full harmonic scale of water.

Mahaffie Stagecoach Stop and Farm Historic Site

The Mahaffie Stagecoach Stop is the only working stagecoach stop that remains on the Santa Fe Trail. Visitors can learn about life on the Kansas frontier, stagecoach travel, and 1860s farming techniques. A favorite activity is riding in the farm's reproduction "Concord" or "mud-wagon" stagecoaches, but the living history productions, livestock, and daily special events also provide guests with a full experience of life in the 1800s. The farm was originally owned by James B. and Lucinda Mahaffie, who purchased it in 1857 and lived there until they retired from farming in the mid-1880s. Travelers began using the farm as a stop on their way west as early as 1858, but by 1864, it was a formal stop on the stagecoach route.

Best Time to Visit: The farm is open Monday through Saturday from 10:00 a.m. to 4:00 p.m.

Pass/Permit/Fees: Admission on Monday and Tuesday is $3 for adults and $2 for children ages 5 to 11. From Wednesday through Saturday, admission is $7 for adults and $5 for children ages 5 to 11. Children ages 4 and under are free.

Closest City or Town: Olathe

Address: 1200 E. Kansas City Rd., Olathe, KS 66061

GPS Coordinates: 38.89286° N, 94.79945° W

Did You Know? Lucinda Mahaffie and her daughters served between 50 to 100 meals to travelers each day.

Stone Pillar Vineyard and Winery

Owned and operated by the Hoff Family, the land upon which the Stone Pillar Vineyard and Winery is built has been in their hands since before the Civil War. However, it's only been a vineyard and winery since 2010 following a vacation that George and Brandi Hoff enjoyed at Niagara on the Lake on a winery tour. The idea of a winery allowed the Hoffs to keep their Kansas land productive even as the city continued to buy up nearby fields and pastures. They planted the first grapevines in 2007 and had delicious wine on the shelves three years later. Their Kansas wine is truly a local product, as they work closely with their own fields and with Kansas growers to produce their high-quality wine. It currently offers sixteen varieties in its winery and for sale.

Best Time to Visit: The winery is open Wednesday and Thursday from 1:00 p.m. to 7:00 p.m., Friday and Saturday from 12:00 p.m. to 8:00 p.m., and on Sunday from 12:00 p.m. to 6:00 p.m.

Pass/Permit/Fees: There is no fee to visit, but be sure to bring money for tastings.

Closest City or Town: Olathe

Address: 11000 S. Woodland St., Olathe, KS 66061

GPS Coordinates: 38.92944° N, 94.81792° W

Did You Know? The winery hosts Friday Night Music, a concert series that is priced starting at $5 per person. Concerts are from 7:00 p.m. to 10:00 p.m., and food trucks and wines from Stone Pillar Vineyard are available.

Flint Hills Nature Trail

At 117 miles in length, the Flint Hills Nature Trail is the seventh-longest rail-trail in the U.S. The trailhead starts in Osawatomie in the east and ends in Herington in the west. It passes through numerous communities, including Ottawa, Vassar, Osage City, Bushong, and Council Grove. The scenic Flint Hills are the backdrop for this trail. That area is among the last remaining tallgrass-prairie ecosystems left in the world.

Along the route, visitors will be treated to national historic sites, several recreational areas, and of course, stunning views. The trail follows the Marais Des Cygnes River in portions of the eastern section, taking travelers past rushing waters, rolling farmland, and towering bluffs.

Best Time to Visit: The best time to visit the Flint Hills Nature Trail is during the spring when the river is full and the wildflowers are in bloom.

Pass/Permit/Fees: There is no fee to visit this location.

Closest City or Town: Osawatomie

Address: 1400 South St., Osawatamoie, KS 66064

GPS Coordinates: 38.49584° N, 94.97893° W

Did You Know? The Flint Hills Trail follows a defunct railroad corridor, which was originally built in the late 1880s. The Council Grove, Osage City & Ottawa Railway (later the Missouri Pacific Railroad) traveled this route until service was discontinued in the 1980s.

1950s All Electric House

The All Electric House in Olathe was a family home for four decades before it became an exhibit for tourists. It is part of the Johnson County Museum and a draw for both children of the 1950s and new generations. The structure was originally built by the Kansas City Power & Light electric company in 1954 as a model home in Prairie Village. Its modern features like a hidden television, garage-door opener, year-round air conditioner, electric curtain opener, and other "futuristic" amenities attracted more than 62,000 visitors the year it opened. At the time, this number was equal to the entire population of Johnson County. This house represented the American Dream for many people in the 1950s and serves as an example of their aspirations.

Best Time to Visit: The museum is open Monday through Saturday from 9:00 a.m. to 4:30 p.m., but you may want to consider free days, which occur once a quarter.

Pass/Permit/Fees: Adult admission is $6 per person, and seniors over the age of 60 are $5. Children ages 1 to 17 are $4, and infants under age 1 are free.

Closest City or Town: Overland Park

Address: 8788 Metcalf Ave, Overland Park, KS 66212

GPS Coordinates: 38.97027° N, 94.66845° W

Did You Know? When you tour the house, take note of other electric gadgets like the foot pedal that opens the fridge, the switch that turns on the coffee pot, and the painting that slides back to reveal a television.

Deanna Rose Children's Farmstead

Established in 1978, the Deanna Rose Children's Farmstead was established to offer a turn-of-the-century farm experience to children in Kansas. Approximately 250 animals and birds of prey call the farm home, and there are also several gardens, a one-room schoolhouse, a fishing pond, pony rides, and many other activities to participate in on the 12-acre property. Additionally, you can find extra activities, programs, and attractions that help visitors learn about wildlife, farm life, and Kansas history. The farm began with just two miniature horses, nine goats, two Shetland ponies, six sheep, twelve chickens, three calves, a single vegetable garden, a child-sized replica of a barn and loft, and a silo with a slide. Over four decades, it has evolved into a popular area attraction that sees more than 400,000 visitors each year.

Best Time to Visit: The farm is open between May and October. Hours are Monday through Sunday from 9:00 a.m. to 4:00 p.m.

Pass/Permit/Fees: Admission is $3 per person. After 2:00 p.m. Monday through Thursday, admission is free.

Closest City or Town: Overland Park

Address: 13800 Switzer Rd., Overland Park, KS 66221

GPS Coordinates: 38.87846° N, 94.70313° W

Did You Know? The farm is named for Deanna Sue Rose, who was the first Overland Park police officer and first female officer in Kansas to die in the line of duty. She was killed in 1985 while she was trying to arrest a suspect.

Overland Park Farmers' Market

A public gathering at the Matt Ross Community Center brings shoppers of all ages together at the Overland Park Farmers' Market. This market has been operating for more than 35 years, providing fresh produce, specialty products, and local foods to Overland Park residents and visitors.

Over 80 local vendors attend, including rural farmers, urban farmers, bakers, dairy farmers, and others. They set up shop on Wednesdays and Saturdays to sell their wares. The goal of the market is to help people find in-season, local foods and support their community at the same time.

At the nearby clocktower pavilion, live music and other performing artists take the stage and provide entertainment to shoppers on market days.

Best Time to Visit: The market is open on Wednesdays and Saturdays from 7:30 a.m. to 1:00 p.m.

Pass/Permit/Fees: There is no fee to visit, but be sure to bring money for shopping.

Closest City or Town: Overland Park

Address: 8101 Marty St., Overland Park, KS 66204

GPS Coordinates: 38.98265° N, 94.66922° W

Did You Know? *Cooking Light* and *Tripping* have both named the Overland Park Farmers' Market as the "Best Farmers' Market in Kansas."

iFLY Kansas City

iFLY is an indoor skydiving experience that allows visitors to experience the thrill of skydiving without having to jump out of an airplane. The first iFLY facility was opened in Orlando in 1998 as a fulfillment of the founder's dream to "empower humans to experience the freedom and thrill of flying." Since then, the company has expanded to eighty worldwide locations, including this one in the Kansas City area.

The technology that produces the flying sensation is eco-friendly wind tunnels that recirculate air and control its speed to lift humans off the ground. The activity is excellent for people aged three and up as long as they're in good health. You don't have to be an athlete, but you do need to be free of back and heart issues.

Best Time to Visit: iFLY is open Thursday, Friday, and Sunday from 11:00 a.m. to 5:00 p.m. and on Saturday from 10:00 a.m. to 7:00 p.m.

Pass/Permit/Fees: A two-flight standard package is $74.99 per person. For each additional flight, a discount will apply.

Closest City or Town: Overland Park

Address: 10975 Metcalf Ave., Overland Park, KS 66210

GPS Coordinates: 38.93094° N, 94.66637° W

Did You Know? The additional purchase of a high flight allows visitors to fly higher and faster with an instructor than on a regular flight. This high flight occurs on one of the two flights that come with the basic flight package.

Indian Creek Hike and Bike Trail

If you traverse the entire length of the Indian Creek Hike and Bike Trail, you'll travel through two states, several parks, and four communities. It is a connection point for numerous areas surrounding the Blue River in Kansas City, Missouri and the Indian Creek in Overland Park, Kansas. For this reason, it's a popular trail for commuters and recreational users. The trail begins in Kansas City, Missouri and extends west across the Missouri–Kansas border into the 66-acre Leawood City Park. Here, you'll find soccer fields and baseball fields, and courts for tennis, basketball, and volleyball. The trail then passes through several neighborhood parks in Overland Park, under Interstate 435, and across the Ottawa University campus. Eventually, you'll enter Olathe, Kansas, winding through dense woodlands before crossing MidAmerica Nazarene University's Campus and entering Southdowns Park. The trail finally comes to an end at Hampton Park in Olathe, Kansas.

Best Time to Visit: This trail is used year-round, but if you're using it for hiking, spring and fall are the best times to avoid the heat of summer.

Pass/Permit/Fees: There is no fee to visit this area.

Closest City or Town: Overland Park

Address: W. 110th Street, Overland Park, KS 66210

GPS Coordinates: 38.89657° N, 94.76067° W

Did You Know? The full length of the Indian Creek Hike and Bike Trail is 26 miles.

Johnson County Museum

In 1967, the Johnson County Museum got its start as an all-volunteer endeavor that was driven by the mission to collect, preserve, and share Johnson County's history with the local community. It was originally housed in a two-room schoolhouse built in 1927, but it moved into its new, larger home, the Johnson County Arts & Heritage Center, in 2017. In addition to its permanent collection of historic artifacts that tell Johnson County's story, the museum offers numerous programs for both children and adults. For instance, adults can enjoy a behind-the-scenes museum tour, the "Scandal in the Schoolhouse" escape room, History on Tap, and the Lunch & Learn Series. Kids can experience Kids' Day Out, Retro Storytime, and Sensory-Friendly Mondays.

Best Time to Visit: The museum is open Monday through Saturday from 9:00 a.m. to 4:30 p.m., but you may want to consider free days, which occur once a quarter. Check the website for dates.

Pass/Permit/Fees: Adult admission is $6 per person, and seniors over the age of 60 are $5. Children ages 1 to 17 are $4, and infants under age 1 are free.

Closest City or Town: Overland Park

Address: 8788 Metcalf Ave., Overland Park, KS 66212

GPS Coordinates: 38.97004° N, 94.66879° W

Did You Know? The Johnson County Museum has received more than 20 awards.

Nerman Museum of Contemporary Art

Since opening in 2007, the Nerman Museum of Contemporary Art is a major provider of visual arts in the region. Located on the Johnson County Community College, this museum receives over 100,000 visitors each year and is an integral part of the community. The building in which the museum is located was designed by architect Kyu Sung Woo and primarily constructed of Kansas limestone. There are eleven large galleries on two levels that house the museum's permanent collection and display the temporary exhibits that rotate in and out of the galleries. Other features at the museum include the 200-seat Hudson Auditorium, two classrooms, a space for art storage, and Café Tempo.

Best Time to Visit: The museum is open Tuesday, Friday, and Saturday from 10:00 a.m. to 5:00 p.m., Wednesday and Thursday from 10:00 a.m. and 8:00 p.m., and Sunday from 12:00 p.m. to 5:00 p.m.

Pass/Permit/Fees: There is no fee to visit the museum.

Closest City or Town: Overland Park

Address: 12345 College Blvd., Overland Park, KS 66210

GPS Coordinates: 38.92559° N, 94.72682° W

Did You Know? In the lobby of the cantilever entrance, you'll find a stunning art installation by Leo Villareal that features 60,000 white LED bulbs. While there are two entrances to the museum, the cantilever entrance is the only one that will allow you to view this incredible work of art.

Old World Balloonery

If you've ever wanted to soar above the world in a hot air balloon, the Old World Balloonery has you covered. As one of the oldest hot air balloon ride companies in the country (established in 1975), you can be sure its pilots have years of experience. Owner and operator Jason Jones has been involved in ballooning since he was five years old when he served as the chase crew for his mother's flights.

Since that time, Jones has logged over 1,000 hours as the main pilot of hot air balloons all over the country. Various balloon rides are available, including group rides, couples' rides, and even tethered rides at fairs and festivals. No matter which ride you choose, you're sure to get some of the most breathtaking views of Kansas City.

Best Time to Visit: Flights need to be scheduled, so contact the company directly at 913-338-2628 to determine the best time for a flight.

Pass/Permit/Fees: Balloon rides start at $200 per person for a group flight.

Closest City or Town: Overland Park

Address: 12600 W. 142nd St., Overland Park, KS 66221

GPS Coordinates: 38.87200° N, 94.73262° W

Did You Know? All hot air balloon passengers at Old World Balloonery must be at least ten years old and able to climb in and out of the basket without assistance. As such, this is not an activity that can be done if you have small children or disabled guests in your group.

Topgolf

Topgolf is a sports entertainment center that provides a high-tech golf game to visitors of all ages and abilities. By renting a bay, you can drive golf balls onto a specially designed course and then use proprietary technology to track your ball and score each shot based on the target it hits.

Up to six players can rent a bay, but only one person should be hitting the ball at a time to make sure the game remains safe. The climate-controlled hitting bays combined with a full food and beverage menu make this an activity that can be enjoyed any time of the year for any occasion.

Best Time to Visit: Topgolf is open Monday through Thursday from 10:00 a.m. to 11:00 p.m., Friday and Saturday from 10:00 a.m. to 12:00 p.m., and Sunday from 10:00 a.m. and 11:00 p.m.

Pass/Permit/Fees: The fee to rent a bay at Topgolf varies based on the time you want to play. Between open and 12:00 p.m., the cost is $27 per hour, per bay. From 12:00 p.m. to 5:00 p.m., the cost is $37 per hour, per bay, and from 5:00 p.m. to close, the cost is $49 per hour, per bay.

Closest City or Town: Overland Park

Address: 10611 Nall Ave, Overland Park, KS 66207

GPS Coordinates: 38.93726° N, 94.64809° W

Did You Know? The same technology that allows you to track your golf ball at Topgolf will tell workers that the ball has left the playing area.

Old Oxford Mill and Restaurant

Built in 1874 along the banks of the Arkansas River, the Oxford Mill operated for 123 years before shutting down in 1997. It had two locations, the first of which was right next to the river. The second was moved to street level when more space was required following the Great Depression. Between 1874 and 1918, the mill changed owners several times before Charles Champeny purchased it and kept it in the family for three generations until the mill closed.

Wallace Champeny, the great-grandson of Charles, restored the original mill in 2000 and opened a restaurant to bring in tourists. The restaurant closed in 2006, but two years later, the Oxford High School Entrepreneurship Program took over restaurant operations for one meal a week on Sundays at 2:00 p.m.

Best Time to Visit: If you want to eat in the restaurant, the only time to visit is on Sunday at 2:00 p.m. The grounds are open to the public for tours during the week.

Pass/Permit/Fees: There is no fee to visit the grounds, but the meals are between $9 and $12 per person, plus $1 for a beverage.

Closest City or Town: Oxford

Address: E 20th Ave N, Oxford, KS 67119

GPS Coordinates: 37.28893° N, 97.16134° W

Did You Know? The mill produced flour and cornmeal under the slogan "Oxford's Best."

Hillsdale State Park

Located just south of Kansas City, Hillsdale State Park is home to 12,000 acres of wildlife and recreational areas. The 4,500-acre lake is full of largemouth bass, walleye, crappie, bluegill, and catfish, which make this park a top choice for anglers, who can fish on the water or along 51 miles of shoreline. Hunting is also allowed here, with 7,000 acres available for this sport.

You're likely to spot whitetail deer, squirrels, rabbits, bobwhite quail, muskrats, and various species of waterfowl. The park is also ideal for birdwatchers, who can find shorebirds, warblers, finches, sparrows, hawks, and even bald eagles roosting in the area. For equestrians, there are 32 miles of marked trails in the Saddle Ridge area east of the reservoir designed specifically for horseback riding.

Best Time to Visit: Visit Hillsdale State Park during hunting season or in the summer for fishing.

Pass/Permit/Fees: There is no fee to visit this location.

Closest City or Town: Richland

Address: Hillsdale State Park, Richland, KS 66071

GPS Coordinates: 38.65767° N, 94.92470° W

Did You Know? When the reservoir at Hillside State Park was created in 1982, more than 70 percent of the standing timber in the area was left to serve as an underwater habitat.

Rolling Hills Zoo

Accredited by the Association of Zoos and Aquariums, Rolling Hills Zoo is dedicated to education, conservation, and animal welfare. It offers its animals enclosures that are as close to their natural environments as possible, and the facility participates in conservation efforts at the local, national, and international levels. Science education programming is available to the public, along with opportunities to learn about the animals through close-encounter events. The zoo got its start when Charlie Walker purchased a tract of land in western Salina County in the 1980s and began showing Belgian horses at his Rolling Hills Ranch to local schoolchildren. He added additional animals to the barn over time, and other locals began requesting to visit his ranch. Together, Charlie and the Salina community established a wildlife park.

Best Time to Visit: The zoo is open daily from 9:00 a.m. to 5:00 p.m.

Pass/Permit/Fees: Adult admission is $13.95 per person, and children between the ages of 3 and 12 are $7 per person. Seniors ages 65 and older are $12.95, and children ages 2 and under are free.

Closest City or Town: Salina

Address: 625 N. Hedville Rd., Salina, KS 67401

GPS Coordinates: 38.85324° N, 97.76424° W

Did You Know? The exotic animal part of the operation separated from the ranch in 1995 and became a private nonprofit organization.

Lake Scott State Park

As one of the most historic locations in Kansas, visitors to Lake Scott State Park will not only find numerous outdoor activities to do but will also get a history lesson as well. In and around the park, there are over twenty-six archeological sites that document the remains of a Native American pueblo (El Cuartelejo), a dwelling of the original settlers on land where the park now stands (the Steele home), and the site of the last Native American battle in the state (Battle Canyon). Even if you're not interested in the history of the area, you can camp, boat, hike, hunt, swim, fish, and watch for wildlife in the park, making it an awesome place for everyone in the family. There is even a horse camp that offers visitors amenities for their four-legged companions. Scott State Fishing Lake is 100 acres and provides an ample stock of channel catfish, crappie, largemouth bass, sunfish, and saugeye.

Best Time to Visit: Visit in the summer for water activities and spring or fall for all others.

Pass/Permit/Fees: There is a $5 fee per vehicle to visit the park.

Closest City or Town: Scott City

Address: 101 W. Scott Lake Dr., Scott City, KS 67871

GPS Coordinates: 38.68603° N, 100.92526° W

Did You Know? *National Geographic* named Lake Scott State Park as one of the country's "50 Must-See State Parks" for its early American history, deep canyons, natural springs, and craggy bluffs.

Cowley Lake

Cowley Lake is an 84-acre, 32-foot-deep fishing lake that contains largemouth bass, redear sunfish, channel catfish, walleye, crappie, flathead, and bluegill fish. While the lake wasn't always a popular fishing spot, in 1988, it was drained and rehabilitated to include fish attractors and other improvements. It was refilled in the spring of 1989, and with the superior water quality and stock, it became a favorite fishing hole for local and visiting anglers. On the 113 acres surrounding the lake, hunting is allowed, but game on the property is typically small (waterfowl, rabbits, quail, and squirrel). The lake is also popular for birdwatching and photography, particularly due to the gorgeous 25-foot waterfall located on the west end of the lake.

Best Time to Visit: The best time to visit Cowley Lake is during the spring and summer.

Pass/Permit/Fees: There is no fee to visit this attraction.

Closest City or Town: Spring Creek

Address: Cowley County State Lake, Spring Creek, KS 67005

GPS Coordinates: 37.09929° N, 96.80272° W

Did You Know? The Cowley Lake waterfall is difficult and dangerous to reach, particularly when the rocks are slippery. There is a dirt road you can drive down that is west of the lake's parking lot. That will get you within 100 feet of the bottom of the falls. If you are not an experienced hiker, this might be the best way to view the falls.

Arikaree Breaks

Located on the northern edge of Cheyenne County, the 36-mile Arikaree Breaks is an anomaly among the plains typically associated with Kansas. The Arikaree Breaks, which feature deep ravines, were formed by sand, clay, and silt particles that were deposited by the wind. This combination of materials is called *loess*, and since it was deposited, it has undergone splitting by the tributaries of the Arikaree River and the South Fork Republican River. The breaks extend into Rawlings County to the east and into Colorado to the west. You'll discover several native grasses growing in the area, which provide an excellent source of food for cattle and wildlife. Due to the lack of water, ranchers have had to drill wells miles away and pipe it into the area to make sure their livestock have enough to drink.

Best Time to Visit: The Arikaree Breaks can be visited at any time of the year, but the best time would be during the spring and summer to avoid harsh weather.

Pass/Permit/Fees: There is no fee to visit this area.

Closest City or Town: St. Francis

Address: E. Washington St., Saint Francis, KS 67756

GPS Coordinates: 39.77824° N, 101.80710° W

Did You Know? Two species of sage grow in the Arikaree Breaks that do not grow in any other place in Kansas. There are also sixteen native plants that have been classified as rare in the state.

Tallgrass National Preserve

At one time, tallgrass prairie encompassed more than 170 million acres in North America, but since the 1800s, the majority of it has been tilled for farmland. Less than 4 percent of this prairieland remains today, and most of it is in Kansas. The Tallgrass National Preserve was established in 1996 to protect this valuable ecosystem. It covers 11,000 acres and offers space for activities like hiking, exploring historic buildings, and taking a cell phone tour. During your visit, you'll likely see blooming wildflowers, a bison herd, and plenty of wildlife. Catch-and-release fishing is available in the ponds and Fox Creek. Thirty-seven different fish species have been caught in these waters, which is partly due to the catch-and-release program.

Best Time to Visit: The best time to visit Tallgrass National Preserve is during the spring or fall when the weather is cooler.

Pass/Permit/Fees: There is no fee to visit the preserve.

Closest City or Town: Strong City

Address: 2480B KS-177, Strong City, KS 66869

GPS Coordinates: 38.44330° N, 96.57296° W

Did You Know? The grass in Tallgrass National Preserve reaches its peak height in the fall. It takes the entire spring and summer for it to grow to its tallest point. Grasses that are 6 inches tall in the spring may be over 6 feet tall in the fall, depending on the amount of rain the area receives throughout the growing season.

Wilson State Park

Located in the Smoky Hills region of the state, Wilson State Park is one of Kansas's prominent water recreation areas. The 956-acre park has two main areas, Hell Creek and Otoe, both of which are on the south side of Wilson Reservoir. Camping is available, but day use is more popular with swimmers, boaters, and hikers. For one of the best views of the 9,000-acre Wilson Reservoir and the Kansas prairie beyond it, hike the 2-mile Dakota Trail, which winds around the hills that surround the lake. Bicyclists will prefer the 10-mile scenic Switchgrass Bike Trail, and the Cedar Trail in the Otoe area is ideal for disabled hikers or those who have little experience. Wilson Reservoir is a favorite fishing spot for anglers, with plenty of striped bass and walleye available in the water.

Best Time to Visit: The best time to visit for water activities is during the summer. For other activities, spring and fall are best because of the cooler weather.

Pass/Permit/Fees: There is a $5 fee per vehicle to visit the park.

Closest City or Town: Sylvan Grove

Address: 3 State Park Road, Sylvan Grove, KS 67481

GPS Coordinates: 38.92194° N, 98.50933° W

Did You Know? Wilson State Park is an excellent place for photographers, not only for the scenic views but also for the wildlife. You might be able to spot bobwhite quail, deer, waterfowl, and various songbirds and migratory birds in the area.

Brown v. Board of Education National Historic Site

The Brown v. Board of Education National Historic Site commemorates the landmark 1954 U.S. Supreme Court decision that ruled in favor of an African American girl who wanted to attend an all-white school in her neighborhood, ending legal segregation in U.S. public schools. This unanimous decision by the Supreme Court Justices decreed that the prevailing "separate but equal" doctrine was unconstitutional and a violation of the 14th Amendment. This historic site is located at the Monroe Elementary School, which was one of four schools designated for black children in Topeka. You can walk through the school's halls and explore what it must have been like for students to attend a segregated school.

Best Time to Visit: The site is open Tuesday through Saturday from 9:00 a.m. to 5:00 p.m.

Pass/Permit/Fees: There is no fee to visit this attraction.

Closest City or Town: Topeka

Address: 1515 SE Monroe St., Topeka, KS 66612

GPS Coordinates: 39.03860° N, 95.67638° W

Did You Know? The initial purpose of the lawsuit in *Brown v. Board of Education* was to bring to light that segregated schools did not receive equal equipment and facilities compared to white-only schools, but the Supreme Court took their ruling further.

Cedar Crest

Cedar Crest is the name of the official residence of Kansas governors. Originally, the Erasmus Bennett house, located at 8th and Buchanan, served this purpose between 1901 and 1962. Cedar Crest has a French-Norman style and was built in 1928. It was named Cedar Crest for its overlook of the Kansas River Valley, which was once filled with cedar trees.

Frank Pitts and Madge MacLennan, the original owners of the land and house, willed the property to the state of Kansas to be used for the governor's residence. When Madge passed away in 1955, the Bennett mansion was in such poor condition that they accepted the gift of Cedar Crest and renamed the land MacLennan Park. In addition to the house, MacLennan also left the state 1,500 books in the library.

Best Time to Visit: The residence is open for tours on Monday only between 1:00 p.m. and 3:30 p.m.

Pass/Permit/Fees: There is no fee to visit this attraction.

Closest City or Town: Topeka

Address: 1 SW Cedar Crest Rd., Topeka, KS 66606

GPS Coordinates: 39.06680° N, 95.74677° W

Did You Know? Republican Governor John Anderson and his family became the last residents in the Bennett mansion and the first to live in Cedar Crest. While Cedar Crest is the smallest governor's residence in the nation at 6,000 square feet, it is situated on the largest plot of land (244 acres).

Combat Air Museum

The Combat Air Museum is one of only a few major aviation museums that is located on an active airfield, which means you will probably witness Air Force fighter aircraft and Army helicopters flying in and out of the area on the day you visit. Forbes Field has the longest runway in Kansas, so there could also be a refueling tanker aircraft from the Kansas Air National Guard on the tarmac as well. In addition to active aircraft, you will also see forty-five stationary aircraft from the earliest days of flying until today. The museum boasts the largest collection of WWI replica aircraft of any air museum in the Midwest. Plus, there are numerous other exhibits that showcase historic aircraft engines, aviation artifacts, and military aviation artwork.

Best Time to Visit: From March through December, the museum is open Monday through Saturday from 9:00 a.m. to 4:30 p.m. and on Sunday from 12:00 p.m. to 4:30 p.m. In January and February, it is open Monday through Sunday from 12:00 p.m. to 4:30 p.m.

Pass/Permit/Fees: Adult admission is $7, and children ages 5 to 17 are $5. Children under the age of 5 are free.

Closest City or Town: Topeka

Address: 7016 SE Forbes Ave., Topeka, KS 66619

GPS Coordinates: 38.94189° N, 95.67801° W

Did You Know? The Combat Air Museum was founded in 1976 as part of the Yesterday's Air Force created by David Tallichet to keep aviation history alive.

92

Evel Knievel Museum

Visitors of all ages will find the Evel Knievel Museum fascinating, as it documents the physics-defying stunts pulled off by the ultimate daredevil, Evel Knievel. Not only will you see the collection of bikes that launched Knievel's career, but you'll also view the legendary 1974 Mack truck and trailer that he affectionately called "Big Red." In the theater, listen to and watch the unbelievable stories about this American icon. Take the virtual reality "jump" to see what it felt like to soar over sixteen vehicles on a motorbike. While you'll never beat Knievel's seventy-five ramp-to-ramp motorcycle jumps, you'll at least be able to see what he saw as he flew over whatever he was jumping, be it cars, canyons, or even sharks.

Best Time to Visit: The museum is open Tuesday through Friday from 10:00 a.m. to 5:00 p.m. and on Saturday from 9:00 a.m. to 5:00 p.m.

Pass/Permit/Fees: Adult admission is $15 per person, and students between the ages of 8 and 16 are $7 per person. Seniors, veterans, and active military members are $12 per person. The virtual reality activity is an additional $5 per person.

Closest City or Town: Topeka

Address: 2047 SW Topeka Blvd., Topeka, KS 66612

GPS Coordinates: 39.03091°N, 95.68236° W

Did You Know? Evel Knievel was uninsurable and was turned down by Lloyd's of London for life insurance thirty-seven times.

Gage Park

Gage Park is a 160-acre park that has a multitude of activities for visitors to enjoy. There is a historic mini train and carousel to ride, a zoo to explore, the historic Reinisch Rose Garden to view, and a 2-mile fitness loop trail to hike. You can also visit the Kansas Children's Discovery Center and the Blaisdell Family Aquatic Center while you're there. At the zoo, you can view more than 250 animals in their natural habitats or attend special animal feedings, training sessions, and behind-the-scenes tours.

The rose garden, which has been in the park since 1932, features more than 5,500 rose bushes with over 350 types of roses. The Helen Hocker Theater produces a number of adult and youth theatrical performances each year, working with the Bath House Players and the Topeka Youth Players to create memorable theater productions.

Best Time to Visit: The best time to visit Gage Park depends on which attractions you want to see.

Pass/Permit/Fees: The fee to visit Gage Park depends on the specific attraction. Check each attraction's website for fees.

Closest City or Town: Topeka

Address: 635 SW Gage Blvd., Topeka, KS 66606

GPS Coordinates: 39.05491° N, 95.72927° W

Did You Know? The Reinisch Rose Garden once won the "More Beautiful America Contest" held by *Better Homes and Gardens* magazine.

Kansas Children's Discovery Center

This interactive children's museum has the mission of enhancing the lives of children and enriching the community it serves. The Kansas Children's Discovery Center opened in 2011. It's become a favorite attraction for locals because children are allowed to discover, create, explore, and learn through play. Visitors from all fifty states and twenty-three countries have come to the museum to enjoy its 15,000 square feet of indoor exhibits that focus on art, science, construction, careers, and more. There is a special space just for toddlers and babies, and a 4.5-acre Nature Explore Outdoor Classroom. Located in Gage Park, the museum is one of many local activities in the area that are geared toward children.

Best Time to Visit: The museum is open Wednesday, Friday, and Saturday from 9:00 a.m. to 5:00 p.m., on Thursday from 9:00 a.m. to 8:00 p.m., and on Sunday from 12:00 p.m. to 5:00 p.m.

Pass/Permit/Fees: Adult and child admission is $9 per person, and seniors ages 65 and older are $8 per person. Infants under the age of 1 are free.

Closest City or Town: Topeka

Address: 4400 SW 10th Ave., Topeka, KS 66604

GPS Coordinates: 39.05275° N, 95.73348° W

Did You Know? Exhibits at the Kansas Children's Discovery Center include *Illumination Station*, *Lift Yourself*, *Ramp Racing*, *Top City Build*, *Financial Literacy*, *Grain*, *Careers*, and more.

Kansas State Capitol

Formally known as the Kansas Statehouse, the Kansas State Capitol is located in Topeka, which has been the capital of Kansas since before it became a state. The peak of the capitol's dome is taller than the U.S. Capitol, which is 288 feet high. However, the diameter of the Kansas State Capitol is significantly smaller at 50 feet compared with 96 feet for its federal counterpart. Tourists can still trek to the top of the dome at the Kansas State Capitol, something that is prohibited in most other state capitols.

Edward Townsend Mix and John G. Haskell designed the Capitol in 1862, and construction began in 1866. Local limestone from Cottonwood Falls was used to build the East and West wings. The central building and dome were not completed until 1903, which means this structure was under construction for thirty-seven years. The sculpture on top of the dome, a Kansa Native American with his bow and arrow pointed at the North Star, was added in 2002.

Best Time to Visit: The Kansas State Capitol is open Monday through Friday from 8:00 a.m. to 5:00 p.m. and on Saturday from 10:00 a.m. to 4:00 p.m.

Pass/Permit/Fees: There is no fee to visit this attraction.

Closest City or Town: Topeka

Address: SW 8th & SW Van Buren St., Topeka, KS 66612

GPS Coordinates: 39.04932° N, 95.67792° W

Did You Know? There are 296 steps between the fifth floor of the capitol and the top of the dome.

Lake Shawnee

With more than 1 million visitors each year, Lake Shawnee is a hugely popular recreational area located in Topeka. It hosts numerous festivals and tournaments every year, but outdoor enthusiasts flock to the lake even if there's no special event happening. Lake Shawnee Adventure Cove is a swim area and floating playground that provides hours of fun for children of all ages.

Along the shoreline of Lake Shawnee, you'll find the Bettis Family Sports Complex, complete with lighted baseball fields, a lighted multi-purpose field, two concession stands, locker rooms, a reception area, conference rooms, and the Lake Shawnee Event Center. Fishing is by far the favorite activity available at the lake, so much so that there's even a heated fishing dock for winter fishing.

Best Time to Visit: The best time to visit Lake Shawnee is during the summer for water activities, late spring for the gardens, and winter for the heated fishing dock.

Pass/Permit/Fees: There is no fee to visit the area, but some individual activities may have separate costs.

Closest City or Town: Topeka

Address: 3137 SE 29th St., Topeka, KS 66605

GPS Coordinates: 39.01149° N, 95.61651° W

Did You Know? Over 5,000 anglers arrived to fish in Lake Shawnee on its opening day in 1939.

Mulvane Art Museum

One of the oldest art museums west of the Mississippi River, the Mulvane Art Museum boasts a collection of about 5,500 works of art from around the world, including prints, sculptures, drawings, paintings, decorative art, and photographs. Named for Joab R. Mulvane, one of the most successful Kansans in the 19th century, the art museum focuses on works from local artists and those in the entire Mountain Plains region. It also frequently features international art, particularly as temporary exhibitions throughout the year. In addition to its art exhibits, the museum also has an education program in visual arts that offers outreach services to students at local public and private schools throughout the area. More than 50,000 visitors come to the museum each year.

Best Time to Visit: The museum is open Tuesday from 12:00 p.m. to 7:00 p.m. and Wednesday through Friday from 12:00 p.m. to 5:00 p.m.

Pass/Permit/Fees: There is no fee to visit the museum.

Closest City or Town: Topeka

Address: 1700 SW Jewell Ave., Topeka, KS 66621

GPS Coordinates: 39.03677° N, 95.70296° W

Did You Know? The original building that housed the museum was destroyed by a tornado in 1966, which allowed the builders to connect the Mulvane Art Museum to the Garvey Fine Arts Center on the Washburn University campus.

Old Prairie Town at Ward-Meade Historic Site

At the Old Prairie Town at Ward-Meade Historic Site, you'll get to explore a village from the 1800s. It features a replica of the 1854 log cabin that served as the home of pioneer Anthony Ward and his family. Ward lived in a cabin like this while his Ward-Meade mansion was being constructed nearby. Other buildings in the village include the 1891 Victor Schoolhouse (and outhouse), the 1880 Everest Church, Mulvane General Store (where the Visitors Center is located), Potwin Drug Store (complete with the Durst Physician's Office and Fyler Dentist Office), Lingo Livery Stable (where you'll also find Landau Carriage and Baughman Ice Cream Wagon), Lingo Tack Shop, Pauline Depot and Caboose, and a turn-of-the-century barbershop. Don't forget to take a stroll through the 2.5-acre Botanical Garden as well.

Best Time to Visit: The site is open from 8:00 a.m. to dusk every day.

Pass/Permit/Fees: Guided tours are available for $5 per adult, $4 per senior, and $3 for children between the ages of 6 and 12. Children ages 5 and under are free.

Closest City or Town: Topeka

Address: 124 NW Fillmore St., Topeka, KS 66606

GPS Coordinates: 39.06420° N, 95.68344° W

Did You Know? Enjoy a family-style hearth meal at the Ward Cabin for $20 per guest.

Ted Ensley Gardens

On the west side of Lake Shawnee, you'll find the Ted Ensley Gardens, a 37.5-acre garden area that features 1,200 varieties of perennials, 300 varieties of annuals, various trees and shrubs, and a gorgeous panoramic view of the lake. The Meditation Garden includes a gazebo, pergola, and pagoda where you can relax and take in the solitude. The water and rock gardens offer peaceful escapes as well. Visitors can take a hike on the paved walking trails and stop to rest on the ADA-accessible deck. The arboretum on the property features 400 total trees from eighty-seven varieties, some of which are rare to see in Kansas. One special tree you'll see is a zelkova tree that will eventually be more than 100 feet tall. The gardens were named for former Shawnee County Parks and Recreation Department employee and county commissioner Ted Ensley.

Best Time to Visit: The gardens are open daily from 6:00 a.m. to 11:00 p.m., but the best time to visit is in April, when the tulips are in bloom.

Pass/Permit/Fees: There is no fee to visit the gardens.

Closest City or Town: Topeka

Address: 3650 SE West Edge Rd., Topeka, KS 66605

GPS Coordinates: 39.00238° N, 95.63387° W

Did You Know? Every April, the Ted Ensley Gardens are one of three locations in the area that celebrate Tulip Time, an annual festival of the Shawnee County Parks and Recreation, when more than 100,000 tulips are planted in the gardens.

Topeka Civic Theatre & Academy

The Topeka Civic Theatre & Academy was founded in 1936 and is the oldest continuously operating community dinner theatre in the United States. In 1999, the theatre moved into the former Gage Elementary School, a 1929 building that honors the architecture and design from when the theatre first opened. The Sheffel Theatre is home to live entertainment such as plays, musicals, and comedy shows. It's named for benefactor Irv Sheffel. The Oldfather Theatre, which houses the stage for the academy, the Theatre for Young Audiences, and studio productions, is named for Charley Oldfather. Additionally, the Helen Hocker Theater in Gage Park is managed by the Topeka Civic Theatre & Academy and hosts a variety of community programming throughout the year.

Best Time to Visit: The best time to visit is when there is a show on stage that you want to see. Check the website for showtimes and dates.

Pass/Permit/Fees: The fee to visit the Topeka Civic Theatre & Academy depends on your show and seat selection.

Closest City or Town: Topeka

Address: 3028 SW 8th Ave, Topeka, KS 66606

GPS Coordinates: 39.05641° N, 95.71484° W

Did You Know? The theatre offers several awards each year, including the Marge Selby, Theatre in the Park, the Waldo B. Heywood, and the TNT awards.

Topeka Performing Arts Center

Originally opening as the Municipal Auditorium in 1940, the Topeka Performing Arts Center has a long history in the city. It has hosted various events, including circuses, sporting events, Broadway productions, and trade shows. The facility underwent a renovation in the 1980s that turned the venue into a state-of-the-art performing arts center, and the name was changed to reflect its new direction in 1991. The main theater can hold 2,417 attendees during the center's live-entertainment performances. A smaller theater, the Hussey Black Box Theatre, has a capacity of 120 and hosts more intimate events. There are also several smaller event spaces that can be reserved for banquets, meetings, and receptions. The Topeka Performing Arts Center also offers free live-art performance classes for local students and a space for community events like ballets, graduations, and dance recitals.

Best Time to Visit: The best time to visit is when there is a performance on stage that you want to see. Check the website for shows, times, and dates.

Pass/Permit/Fees: The fee to visit the Topeka Performing Arts Center depends on your show and seat selection.

Closest City or Town: Topeka

Address: 214 SE 8th Ave, Topeka, KS 66603

GPS Coordinates: 39.05000° N, 95.67221° W

Did You Know? About 75,000 people visit the Topeka Performing Arts Center annually.

Topeka Zoo & Conservation Center

The Topeka Zoological Park was established in 1933 and renamed the Topeka Zoo & Conservation Center in 2016 to better represent its mission. As a facility accredited by the Association of Zoos and Aquariums (AZA), the zoo strives to provide enrichment to the community through wildlife education and conservation. Major exhibits include *Animals and Man, Tropical Rainforest, Discovering Apes, Lions Pride, Children's Zoo, Hills' Black Bear Woods, Jungle Cats, Kansas Carnivores, Adventure Trails,* the *Lorikeet Feeding Aviary*, and the *Butterfly Pavilion*. The zoo works in cooperation with the AZA Species Survival Plan to manage specific species that are threatened or endangered.

Best Time to Visit: The zoo is open daily from 9:00 a.m. to 5:00 p.m., with the latest entrance at 4:30 p.m. Some animals will not be on display, depending on the season you visit.

Pass/Permit/Fees: Adult admission is $8.75, and seniors ages 65 and older are $7.75. Children between the ages of 3 and 12 are $7.25, and children ages 2 and under are free.

Closest City or Town: Topeka

Address: 635 SW Gage Blvd, Topeka, KS 66606

GPS Coordinates: 39.05874° N, 95.72519° W

Did You Know? Zoo guests can learn how to catch, tag, and release monarch butterflies during their annual September migration through Kansas.

The Cathedral of the Plains

The Basilica of St. Fidelis, also known as The Cathedral of the Plains, is a minor basilica in the Catholic faith that was placed on the National Register of Historic Places in 1971. It was named as one of the Eight Wonders of Kansas in 2008 after a public vote. The church was designated a minor basilica by Pope Francis in 2014, making it the first basilica in Kansas and the 78th overall in the United States.

Construction on the basilica began in 1908 and was completed in 1911. It is made from native local limestone that was quarried just 7 miles south of Victoria. The Romanesque design is in the form of a cross, and it features two magnificent towers, a rose window, and a stone statue of St. Fidelis. At capacity, the church can seat 1,100 worshippers, making it the largest church west of the Mississippi River at the time of its dedication.

Best Time to Visit: You can visit the church at any time, but if you want to attend Mass, it is held on Saturday at 5:00 p.m. and on Sunday at 10:00 a.m.

Pass/Permit/Fees: There is no fee to visit the cathedral.

Closest City or Town: Victoria

Address: 900 Cathedral, Victoria, KS 67671

GPS Coordinates: 38.85714° N, 99.15096° W

Did You Know? More than 16,000 visitors come to see the basilica each year. It is open during daylight hours for a self-guided audio tour that begins in the west vestibule of the church.

Oz Museum

The Oz Museum in Wamego is committed to exhibiting artifacts related to *The Wonderful Wizard of Oz* by L. Frank Baum and the subsequent movie adaptation. Since the main character, Dorothy, is from Kansas, it's only logical to have a museum dedicated to her story in a Kansas town. The museum opened in 2003 as a tribute to both the book and the movie and now boasts more than 2,000 artifacts dating back to the year 1900 when Baum wrote the book. You'll find some of the earliest editions of the novel, along with nearly every commercial item ever produced with the Wizard of Oz theme, including board games, PEZ dispensers, dolls, lunch boxes, and much more. Even the trip to the museum is fun as you drive in on "The Road to Oz."

Best Time to Visit: The museum is open Monday through Saturday between 9:00 a.m. and 6:00 p.m. and on Sunday from 12:00 p.m. to 6:00 p.m.

Pass/Permit/Fees: Adult admission is $9 per person, and children ages 3 through 12 are $7.

Closest City or Town: Wamego

Address: 511 Lincoln Ave., Wamego, KS 66547

GPS Coordinates: 39.20326° N, 96.30545° W

Did You Know? Among the most popular artifacts at the museum is the pair of hand-jeweled ruby slippers that are covered in more than 3,500 Swarovski crystals. Artist Jeffery Merrell created them for the 50th anniversary of the movie.

Big Brutus

More than 50 years ago, a giant earth mover worked non-stop to dig into the ground in search of coal. At sixteen stories high and 11 million pounds in weight, Big Brutus mined the southeastern corner of Kansas for this precious material until 1974, when the owner put it out of commission. Rather than dismantle this huge machine, the locals decided to turn it into a museum and have it declared a state landmark. Now, guests are encouraged to climb around inside Big Brutus, exploring the massive corridors and chambers. A 48-star flag can be found in the motor room, and a sign showing its final electric bill ($27,000 in the last month of operation) is posted near the entrance. Visitors can also take the opportunity to learn about the coal mining industry by examining photos of steam shovels and a 6-foot-tall, 1,200-pound model of one that is similar to Brutus. It actually works!

Best Time to Visit: The museum is open daily from 9:00 a.m. to 5:00 p.m.

Pass/Permit/Fees: Adult admission is $8.75, and children between the ages of 6 and 12 are $5.50. Seniors and military members are $8.25.

Closest City or Town: West Mineral

Address: 6509 NW 60th St., West Mineral, KS 66782

GPS Coordinates: 37.27437° N, 94.93844° W

Did You Know? Each bucket of earth that Big Brutus pulled out of the ground could fill three train cars.

Four-State Lookout

As one of the Eight Wonders of Kansas, the Four-State Lookout is one of the premier spots in the state for viewing a panorama of the Missouri River Valley. When the weather is clear, you're able to see parts of four states: Kansas, Missouri, Nebraska, and Iowa. You'll definitely want to bring your camera to capture these breathtaking views. This platform sits atop a hill in the glacial hills region and provides the vantage point for the four-state panoramic view.

Visitors have been coming to this hilltop to view the river below since before the 1930s, when three concrete pillars were erected at the site to mark the directions in which to look to view each state. *Nebraska* and *Iowa* are printed on the north pillar; *Missouri* and *Kansas* are printed on the south pillar. *Four State Lookout White Cloud* is printed on the third pillar.

Best Time to Visit: The best time to visit the Four-State Lookout is when the weather is clear.

Pass/Permit/Fees: There is no fee to visit this area.

Closest City or Town: White Cloud

Address: 3rd St., White Cloud, KS 66094

GPS Coordinates: 39.97932° N, 95.29957° W

Did You Know? The platform for viewing the four states was not built until 2004 when the town was celebrating the bicentennial of the Lewis and Clark Expedition.

Botanica, The Wichita Gardens

Located on 17 acres in downtown Wichita, Botanica provides a slice of nature in the middle of the city. The attraction opened in 1987 with just four gardens, but over the years, it has grown to include a butterfly garden and house, an aquatic garden, a greenhouse for tropical flora, a juniper garden that features over thirty types of junipers, a peony garden, pinetum, a rock garden, a rose garden, a Shakespearean garden, a woodlands garden, and a xeriscape demonstration garden. In 2011, the Downing Children's Garden was added, which features themed areas such as Salamander Stream, Monster Woods, Granddaddy's Musical Maze, and a sunflower and rainbow fountain and plaza.

Best Time to Visit: Botanica is open Monday through Saturday from 9:00 a.m. to 5:00 p.m., but spring and summer are the best times to visit to see the flowers in bloom. Between April and September, the hours are extended to 8:00 p.m. on Tuesday and Thursday.

Pass/Permit/Fees: Adult admission is $10, and seniors and children over the age of 2 are $8. Children ages 2 and under are free.

Closest City or Town: Wichita

Address: 701 Amidon St., Wichita, KS 67203

GPS Coordinates: 37.69699° N, 97.36326° W

Did You Know? Don't forget to ride the 1949 Allan Herschell Company carousel that was placed in the Downing Children's Garden in 2014.

Central Standard Brewing Company

The Central Standard Brewing Company opened in 2015, and it didn't take long for it to start winning awards. It received a silver medal for its Standard Issue Belgian Style Grisette ale at the Great American Beer Festival just a year later. The craft brewery has become a favorite for all kinds of beer, especially since it focuses on using local ingredients whenever possible. Raw Kansas wheat purchased in Yoder and authentic Kansas wildflower honey are just two of the local products that make it into various beers at the brewery. The owners, Andy Boyd and Ian Crane, brewed beer together at home for a decade before they decided to open the brewery. They first tested their beer with their friends and family before developing a business plan in 2010.

Best Time to Visit: The brewery is open Tuesday through Thursday from 3:00 p.m. to 10:00 p.m., Friday from 3:00 p.m. to 12:00 a.m., Saturday from 12:00 p.m. to 12:00 a.m., and Sunday from 12:00 p.m. to 5:00 p.m.

Pass/Permit/Fees: There is no fee to visit Central Standard Brewing Company but be sure to bring some money to try the adult beverages.

Closest City or Town: Wichita

Address: 156 Greenwood, Wichita, KS 67211

GPS Coordinates: 37.68536° N, 97.31856° W

Did You Know? Central Standard Brewing Company won an award in the 2016 Great American Beer Festival, putting it on the map.

Exploration Place

The Exploration Place is also known as the Sedgwick County Science and Discovery Center. It's the top science center in Kansas. The main goal of the center is to inspire a deeper interest in science by creating fun and creative experiences for everyone regardless of age. The concept for the center was developed in 1989, but it took until 2000 before the construction was completed and the exhibits were opened to the public. Permanent exhibits at the center include *Design Build Fly*, *Where Kids Rule*, *Kansas Kids Connect*, *Explore Kansas*, *Bridging Art & Science*, *Kansas in Miniature*, *Nano*, *Making a Landmark*, *Big Mouth*, *Exploration Park*, and more.

Best Time to Visit: The center is open Monday through Wednesday and Friday through Sunday from 10:00 a.m. to 5:00 p.m. On Thursday, it is open from 10:00 a.m. to 8:00 p.m.

Pass/Permit/Fees: Adult admission is $11.50 per person. Children ages 3 to 11 are $8.00, and seniors ages 65 and older are $10.00. Children under age 2 are free.

Closest City or Town: Wichita

Address: 300 N. McLean Blvd., Wichita, KS 67203

GPS Coordinates: 37.69024° N, 97.34812° W

Did You Know? The Digital Dome Theater at the center shows various film and live science shows for an additional cost of $8.00 for adults, $6.00 for children, and $7.00 for seniors. See the museum website for the show schedule.

Frank Lloyd Wright's Allen House

Built in 1918 for owners Henry and Elsie Allen, Frank Lloyd Wright's Allen House was the last of the famous architect's prairie houses, which were designed with earth tones, horizontal lines, and a blending of the interiors and exteriors. Many architectural experts who have visited the house consider the living room to be "one of the great rooms of the 20th century." There are over thirty pieces of furniture designed by Frank Lloyd Wright in the house, and other features like the original art glass and wall-hung water closets make the structure both gorgeous and innovative for its time. The house is a model example of Wright's belief that humans should live in harmony with nature, as there are ponds, gardens, huge windows, and natural colors throughout the property.

Best Time to Visit: Frank Lloyd Wright's Allen House is open Wednesday through Saturday. Tours begin at 10:00 a.m.

Pass/Permit/Fees: The Standard Tour and Moonlight Tour are $22 per person, and the Grand Tour is $40 per person.

Closest City or Town: Wichita

Address: 255 N. Roosevelt St., Wichita, KS 67208

GPS Coordinates: 37.69049° N, 97.29233° W

Did You Know? Elsie Allen, who lived in the house until her death in 1957, was an avid art collector and owned more than 400 works of art. Take the Elsie Allen Art Tour to view the original artwork on display in the house. This tour only provides a "mini-tour" of the house.

Great Plains Nature Center

The Great Plains Nature Center resulted from a joint venture involving the Wichita Department of Parks and Recreation, the Kansas Department of Wildlife, Parks, and Tourism, and the U.S. Fish and Wildlife Service. It was created to provide interpretive, educational, and recreational opportunities to the public. The facility offers a space where visitors of all ages can learn about natural resources, particularly the habitats and wildlife of the Great Plains.

Koch Habitat Hall is a 3,500-square-foot display space that houses exhibits on the prairies, wetlands, rivers, woodlands, climate, effects of European settlement, and wildlife. There is also a 2,200-gallon aquarium that features local fish and rotating live animal exhibits. In the Bob Gress Wildlife Observatory, you'll see a variety of animals, including turkeys, deer, skunks, woodpeckers, and numerous songbirds.

Best Time to Visit: The center is open Monday through Saturday from 9:00 a.m. to 5:00 p.m.

Pass/Permit/Fees: There is no fee to visit this attraction.

Closest City or Town: Wichita

Address: 6232 E. 29th St. N, unit 220, Wichita, KS 67220

GPS Coordinates: 37.74017° N, 97.26387° W

Did You Know? The Kansas Wildlife Exhibit offers eight displays of native reptiles, birds, and mammals. Live feedings are every day at noon.

112

Great Plains Transportation Museum

As the former Great Plains Railway Museum, the Great Plains Transportation Museum has an extensive history in Kansas. The original museum closed in 1977 after losing its space in Union Station as it underwent an extensive renovation. In 1983, a group of railroad enthusiasts incorporated a new museum in Wichita that would feature a Santa Fe locomotive as the main attraction. Additionally, the existing exhibits of a Frisco wooden caboose, a KG&E electric locomotive, and a Santa Fe drover's car would continue to be displayed. The grand opening of the museum occurred in 1986, and the facility continued to acquire new railroad related items to make the museum what it is today. The museum also holds special events such as community group tours, lectures, demonstrations, and temporary exhibits.

Best Time to Visit: The museum is open Saturday from 9:00 a.m. to 4:00 p.m. and on Sunday from 1:00 p.m. to 4:00 p.m. It's open April through October only.

Pass/Permit/Fees: Adult admission is $7 per person. Children between the ages of 4 and 12 are $4, and children ages 3 and under are free.

Closest City or Town: Wichita

Address: 700 E. Douglas Ave., Wichita, KS 67202

GPS Coordinates: 37.68706° N, 97.32948° W

Did You Know? Two annual events held by the Great Plains Transportation Museum are the Trains & Toy Trains Celebration in July and Railfest in October.

Kansas Firefighters Museum

Situated in the 1909 Engine House No. 6 in Wichita, the Kansas Firefighters Museum displays thousands of artifacts related to firefighting in the state, including a Howe hand-pumper from the 1880s, a hand-drawn chemical extinguisher, and a hand-drawn hose reel from the 1800s. There are also authentic vintage firetrucks on exhibit, including a 1928 Model A and 1923 Ford Model T. Other artifacts include badges, uniforms, caps, helmets, hydrants, alarms, nozzles, wooden water mains, ladders, axes, sirens, leather buckets, and hundreds of photographs. You can have your picture taken on a steam pumper and experience ringing the fire bell. Observe the types of beds firefighters used to sleep in when on call at Engine House No. 6, and peer down the hole of the brass fire pole.

Best Time to Visit: The museum is open only on Saturday from 11:00 a.m. to 4:00 p.m.

Pass/Permit/Fees: Adult admission is $3 per person, and students ages 5 and up are $2. Seniors are $2.50, and children ages 4 and under are free.

Closest City or Town: Wichita

Address: 1300 S. Broadway St., Wichita, KS 67211

GPS Coordinates: 37.66991° N, 97.33523° W

Did You Know? Be sure to visit the Memorial Garden south of the museum. The garden features a wall engraved with the names of Kansas firefighters who lost their lives in the line of duty and houses the "Last Call" memorial statue.

Keeper of the Plains

A 44-foot-tall steel sculpture stands at the convergence of the Big and Little Arkansas rivers in downtown Wichita. It appears to watch over the land between the two rivers. This sculpture is called *Keeper of the Plains* as a nod to the sacred land that once belonged to Native Americans. The sculpture was created by artist Blackbear Bosin, a Native American and lifelong Wichita resident. It was constructed in 1974 to celebrate the U.S. bicentennial and has stood watch over the city and plains since then.

Every evening, fire pots that surround the statue, known as the Ring of Fire, are lit, which draw visitors to the sculpture and the two suspended foot bridges that dross the Keeper of the Plains Plaza. After undergoing a renovation several decades after it was first installed, the *Keeper of the Plains* statue now stands 30 feet taller because of a new pedestal that raises it up even higher.

Best Time to Visit: The best time to visit the statue is at 7:00 p.m. in the fall and winter and 9:00 p.m. in the spring and summer to view the lit Ring of Fire.

Pass/Permit/Fees: There is no fee to visit this attraction.

Closest City or Town: Wichita

Address: 339 Veterans Pkwy, Wichita, KS 67203

GPS Coordinates: 37.69196° N, 97.34987° W

Did You Know? The fire pots only burn for fifteen minutes each evening (except in inclement weather or when river levels interfere).

Mid-America All-Indian Museum

Located adjacent to the Arkansas River in downtown Wichita, the Mid-America All-Indian Museum is a cultural organization dedicated to educating visitors and the community about the heritage, art, and culture of Native Americans. It also aims to recognize the critical role the tribes play in society today.

The museum houses more than 3,000 artifacts that are displayed on a rotating schedule throughout the year. This allows the museum to tell as many stories about Native American culture as possible. The Artist Gardens, located between the museum and Keeper Plaza, feature the art of two influential Native American artists: Woody Crumbo and Blackbear Bosin, the latter of whom designed the 44-foot *Keeper of the Plains* statue.

Best Time to Visit: The museum is open Tuesday through Saturday from 10:00 a.m. to 4:00 p.m.

Pass/Permit/Fees: Adult admission is $7 per person, and children ages 6 to 12 are $3 per person. Seniors ages 55 and older, students ages 13 and up (with ID), and military members are $5 per person.

Closest City or Town: Wichita

Address: 650 N. Seneca St., Wichita, KS 67203

GPS Coordinates: 37.69292° N, 97.35196° W

Did You Know? Fittingly, the museum is located under the watchful eye of the *Keeper of the Plains* sculpture, which is located east of the museum in Keeper Plaza.

Museum of World Treasures

Founded in 2001 by Dr. Jon and Lorna Kardatzke, the Museum of World Treasures is a nonprofit organization that offers various educational programs along with fascinating exhibits that feature everything from Egyptian mummies and Roman emperors to Civil War weapons and the prehistoric sea creatures that once patrolled the Western Inland Sea. You could spend hours exploring all the permanent exhibits in the Natural History, Military, American History, and World Civilizations displays, and then there are the rotating galleries as well. Check out the items in the New Treasures Case, the Small Stories Case, and the Real Document Case to see something different every time you visit. For a truly special event, rent the museum's banquet room for a one-of-a-kind setting for a birthday party, business meeting, or wedding.

Best Time to Visit: The museum is open Wednesday through Saturday from 10:00 a.m. to 5:00 p.m. and on Sunday from 12:00 p.m. to 5:00 p.m.

Pass/Permit/Fees: Adult admission is $9.95 per person, and children between the ages of 4 and 12 are $7.95 per person. Seniors ages 65 and older are $8.95, and children ages 3 and under are free.

Closest City or Town: Wichita

Address: 835 E. 1st St. N, Wichita, KS 67202

GPS Coordinates: 37.68797° N, 97.32806° W

Did You Know? The museum contains artifacts from more than 200 different collectors.

Old Cowtown Museum

When you step into Old Cowtown Museum, you step back in time to the mid-1800s. The Chisholm Trail that once passed through the area was called Cowtown. Now, you can explore over 10,000 artifacts that tell the story of Wichita's evolution from a frontier settlement to an agricultural and manufacturing center.

At Cowtown, you can explore twenty-seven historic and recreated structures that are located along the banks of the Arkansas River. Among the original buildings that were relocated to the museum are the Arkansas Valley Grain Elevator & Scale House, the Blood Family Homestead, the City Eagle Print Shop, Empire Hall, Fritz Snitzler's Saloon, the General Store, the Jail, Gardner Coal, Trapper's Cabin, and more.

Best Time to Visit: The museum is open Tuesday through Saturday from 10:00 a.m. to 5:00 p.m. and Sunday from 12:00 p.m. to 5:00 p.m.

Pass/Permit/Fees: Adult admission is $9, and seniors ages 62 and older are $8. Children between the ages of 12 and 17 are $7, and children between the ages of 5 and 11 are $6. Children ages 4 and under are free.

Closest City or Town: Wichita

Address: 1865 Museum Blvd, Wichita, KS 67203

GPS Coordinates: 37.69402° N, 97.35990° W

Did You Know? Wagon rides, gunfight shows, and authentic dress are all included as part of the experience.

118

Orpheum Theater

As the first atmospheric theater in the country, the Orpheum Theater has made its mark in American history. It is currently the oldest atmospheric theater still standing, which is a testament to its construction using the finest materials available in the 1920s. The theater opened in September 1922 and has continued to be the most prominent venue in Wichita for live theater, music, comedy, film, and dance. However, it also serves as a community event center for church services, weddings, lectures, and many other special occasions. It eventually closed in 1976 and was expected to meet the fate of the wrecking ball, but the Orpheum Performing Arts Center, a new nonprofit organization, saved it from demolition and reopened it in 1984.

Best Time to Visit: The best time to visit the Orpheum Theater is when there is a show you want to see. Check the website for showtimes and dates.

Pass/Permit/Fees: The fee to visit the Orpheum Theater depends on your show and seat selection.

Closest City or Town: Wichita

Address: 200 N. Broadway #102, Wichita, KS 67202

GPS Coordinates: 37.68878° N, 97.33530° W

Did You Know? Originally, the theater was intended as a Vaudeville house, but within seven years of opening, it was converted to a movie theater to show "talkies."

Sedgwick County Zoo

The Sedgwick County Zoo houses approximately 3,000 animals from 400 species in settings that replicate their natural geographical habitats. Visit exotic animals from all over the world. The aviary on the property is one of the largest walk-through aviaries in the country. Interactive exhibits make this zoo unique among its kind, as exhibits are designed to immerse visitors in the animals' world. You'll be able to observe the animals' natural behaviors and, in some cases, walk freely among the animals and plants. For an extra charge, you can feed the giraffes, take a boat tour of the zoo, or get up close and personal with elephants.

Best Time to Visit: The zoo is open from 9:00 a.m. to 5:00 p.m. The best time to visit may be when you can view the animals of your choice, so check the website for schedules.

Pass/Permit/Fees: Adult admission is $20 per person. Children between the ages of 3 and 11 and seniors ages 62 and older are $15 per person. Children under the age of 3 are free.

Closest City or Town: Wichita

Address: 5555 W. Zoo Blvd., Wichita, KS 67212

GPS Coordinates: 37.71771° N, 97.40848° W

Did You Know? The zoo has earned numerous national and international awards for its conservation and breeding programs.

The Original Pizza Hut Museum

Kansas may be an unlikely place to be the founding location of one of the most famous pizza chains in the world, but that's exactly what it is for Pizza Hut. The Original Pizza Hut Museum tells the story of brothers Dan and Frank Carney, two Wichita State University students who started the iconic pizza franchise in 1958. They initially had the dream of opening a small pizza place just off the WSU campus, but soon after opening, they expanded their operations to a second shop in Topeka.

In 1986, the building was moved from its original location on Bluff and Kellogg to the WSU campus as a testament to the pizza chain's humble beginnings. You'll notice that the small brick structure looks more like a house than the Pizza Hut buildings of today because the franchise's red, pavilion-style roofs didn't make their debut until the 1960s.

Best Time to Visit: The museum is open Monday through Friday from 11:00 a.m. to 5:00 p.m.

Pass/Permit/Fees: There is no fee to visit the museum.

Closest City or Town: Wichita

Address: 2090 Innovation Blvd., Wichita, KS 67208

GPS Coordinates: 37.72182° N, 97.28662° W

Did You Know? Before Pizza Hut became a national phenomenon, the Carney brothers decided to create a mascot. They came up with Pizza Pete, who wore a checkered bandana around his neck, an apron, hat, and moustache.

Ulrich Museum of Art

Located on the Wichita State University Campus, the Edwin A. Ulrich Museum of Art first opened in 1974 in the McKnight Art Center. There are several works of art that this museum is known for, including the large Joan Miro marble-and-Venetian-glass mosaic that graces the building's façade and the Martin H. Bush Outdoor Sculpture Collection that features eighty sculptures spread across 330 acres. Artists that have sculptures in this garden include Joan Miro, Tom Otterness, Andy Goldworthy, Fernando Botero, Elyn Zimmerman, and more. The museum boasts a permanent collection of 6,500 works of art, including outdoor sculptures. Visitors are treated to 20th and 21st-century art exhibits, both from this permanent collection and in temporary shows that make their way through the museum's rotation.

Best Time to Visit: The museum is open Monday through Saturday from 11:00 a.m. to 5:00 p.m. It is closed on Sundays, major holidays, and university holidays.

Pass/Permit/Fees: There is no fee to visit the museum.

Closest City or Town: Wichita

Address: Wichita State University, 1845 Fairmount St, Wichita, KS 67260

GPS Coordinates: 37.71777° N, 97.29666° W

Did You Know? Of the eleven murals created in his lifetime, the façade mural, *Personnages Oiseaux*, was the only one Miro made out of marble and glass.

Wichita Cathedral

The Wichita Cathedral, formally named the Cathedral of the Immaculate Conception, is a stunning display of architecture from the early 1900s. Designed by architect Emmanuel Louis Masqueray, the cathedral features a rose granite foundation, which was allowed to settle for two years after it was laid before construction continued on the structure itself.

The foundation was put in place in 1906, but the cathedral wasn't completed and opened to the public until 1912. The large granite columns on the front porch are among the most significant details, having come from an old post office in Chicago. They were shipped to Wichita by railroad after the post office was demolished.

Best Time to Visit: If you'd like to attend mass at the Wichita Cathedral, the times are 5:00 p.m. and 7:00 p.m. on Saturday, 8:30 a.m. and 10:00 a.m. on Sunday, 8:00 a.m. on Monday, Wednesday, and Friday, 12:00 p.m. on Monday through Friday, and 6:30 p.m. on Tuesday and Thursday.

Pass/Permit/Fees: There is no fee to visit the cathedral.

Closest City or Town: Wichita

Address: 430 N Broadway, Wichita, KS 67202

GPS Coordinates: 37.69395° N, 97.33536° W

Did You Know? The bronze doors at the front of the cathedral were designed and created by Domus Dei and installed in 1997 as replacements for the original wooden doors.

Wichita-Sedgwick County Historical Museum

Located in Old City Hall, the Wichita-Sedgwick County Historical Museum was founded in 1919 by the Sedgwick County Pioneer Society when Mrs. George Whitney began to collect and house artifacts in the Sedgwick County Courthouse. The actual museum, then named the Wichita Public Museum, was not established until 1938, when the artifacts were moved from the courthouse to the Forum in 1939. The name was changed again to the Wichita Historical Museum Association in 1947, and in 1955, Mrs. Cyrus M. Beachy left her entire collection of antiques and dolls and her house to the association. This endowment led to the creation of the Wichita-Sedgwick County Historical Museum as it stands today. The Old City Hall location opened to the public in 1981.

Best Time to Visit: The museum is open Tuesday through Friday from 11:00 a.m. to 4:00 p.m. and on Saturday and Sunday from 1:00 p.m. to 5:00 p.m.

Pass/Permit/Fees: Adult admission is $5. Children between the ages of 6 and 12 are $2, and children under the age of 6 are free.

Closest City or Town: Wichita

Address: 204

GPS Coordinates: 37.68530° N, 97.33786° W

Did You Know? The museum's permanent collection includes more than 80,000 artifacts.

124

Wichita Toy Train Museum

In 1985, the Wichita Toy Train Museum evolved out of the Wichita Toy Train Club's love of toy trains. Initially, the club intended to build temporary and permanent toy train layouts in places like the Children's Museum of Wichita. Eventually, the cub members decided to open a 1,400-square-foot area dubbed Train Mania in the Pawnee Plaza Mall to display both the Children's Museum layout and a second O-gauge modular layout that had been in storage for years. The display grew so large that the club had to move to a larger suite in the Twin Lakes Mall. They called it Train Mania II. In 2012, the club moved all displays to a permanent home in Wichita and named the new location the Wichita Toy Train Museum.

Best Time to Visit:
The Wichita Toy Train Museum is only open on Saturday from 10:00 a.m. to 5:00 p.m., but it holds numerous special events throughout the year. Check the website for dates and times.

Pass/Permit/Fees: Adult admission is $5. Children ages 12 and under are free with a paying adult.

Closest City or Town: Wichita

Address: 130 S Laura St Ave, Wichita, KS 67211

GPS Coordinates: 37.68574° N, 97.32336° W

Did You Know? The highlighted feature is the Bill Taggart layout of a miniature 19th-century Wichita that includes historic buildings and vintage cars.

Proper Planning

With this guide, you are well on your way to properly planning a marvelous adventure. When you plan your travels, you should become familiar with the area, save any maps to your phone for access without internet, and bring plenty of water—especially during the summer months. Depending on which adventure you choose, you will also want to bring snacks or even a lunch. For younger children, you should do your research and find destinations that best suit your family's needs. You should also plan when and where to get gas, local lodgings, and food. We've done our best to group these destinations based on nearby towns and cities to help make planning easier.

Dangerous Wildlife

There are several dangerous animals and insects you may encounter while hiking. With a good dose of caution and awareness, you can explore safely. Here are steps you can take to keep yourself and your loved ones safe from dangerous flora and fauna while exploring:

- Keep to the established trails.
- Do not look under rocks, leaves, or sticks.
- Keep hands and feet out of small crawl spaces, bushes, covered areas, or crevices.
- Wear long sleeves and pants to keep arms and legs protected.
- Keep your distance should you encounter any dangerous wildlife or plants.

Limited Cell Service

Do not rely on cell service for navigation or emergencies. Always have a map with you and let someone know where you are and how long you intend to be gone, just in case.

First Aid Information

Always travel with a first aid kit in case of emergencies.

Here are items you should be certain to include in your primary first aid kit:

- Nitrile gloves
- Blister care products
- Band-Aids in multiple sizes and waterproof type
- Ace wrap and athletic tape
- Alcohol wipes and antibiotic ointment
- Irrigation syringe
- Tweezers, nail clippers, trauma shears, safety pins
- Small zip-lock bags containing contaminated trash

It is recommended to also keep a secondary first aid kit, especially when hiking, for more serious injuries or medical emergencies. Items in this should include:

- Blood clotting sponges
- Sterile gauze pads
- Trauma pads

- Second-skin/burn treatment
- Triangular bandages/sling
- Butterfly strips
- Tincture of benzoin
- Medications (ibuprofen, acetaminophen, antihistamine, aspirin, etc.)
- Thermometer
- CPR mask
- Wilderness medicine handbook
- Antivenin

There is much more to explore, but this is a great start.

For information on all national parks, visit https://www.nps.gov/index.htm .

This site will give you information on up-to-date entrance fees and how to purchase a park pass for unlimited access to national and state parks. This site will also introduce you to all of the trails at each park.

Always check before you travel to destinations to make sure there are no closures. Some hiking trails close when there is heavy rain or snow in the area and other parks close parts of their land for the migration of wildlife. Attractions may change their hours or temporarily shut down for various reasons. Check the websites for the most up-to-date information.